ALGERIA:
STRUGGLE FOR
TRUTH AND JUSTICE

ALGERIA: STRUGGLE FOR TRUTH AND JUSTICE

A PERSONAL VIEW OF FIFTY YEARS OF MILITARY RULE

ROGER GOLDSMITH

Matador
9 Priory Business Park,
Wistow Road, Kibworth Beauchamp,
Leicestershire. LE8 0RX
Tel: 0116 279 2299
Email: books@troubador.co.uk
Web: www.troubador.co.uk/matador
Twitter: @matadorbooks

ISBN 978 1838594 800

British Library Cataloguing in Publication Data.
A catalogue record for this book is available from the British Library.

Printed and bound in Great Britain by 4edge Limited
Typeset in 11pt Minion Pro by Troubador Publishing Ltd, Leicester, UK

Matador is an imprint of Troubador Publishing Ltd

Dedicated to NASSERA DUTOUR,
who has been fighting for truth and justice in Algeria
since her son Amine 'disappeared' on 30 January 1997

CONTENTS

ACKNOWLEDGEMENTS

This book is the result of interest and research over many years and I have been fortunate to receive much help from many people; academic and Amnesty staff, Algerian friends and others who have helped by reading and offering advice on my manuscripts. Without their assistance and encouragement, the work would not have been completed and I thank them all, whether named here or not. The first reader of the first manuscript was a good friend from Amnesty, Gitti Dunham, who wrote to me that it must be published, a course I had not considered at that time. I thank a number of academic staff and most particularly I thank Richard Gillespie, the second in-depth reader, who made many suggestions and has continued since then to encourage me to publish. Michael Willis made further helpful suggestions. Hugh Roberts picked up important errors I had made in the synopsis I sent him and helpfully suggested that I should develop the book more as a memoir of the early years of independence and of my experience of the terrible years of the 1990s. In addition to these authors, I have made use of many other works, including

French and Algerian sources (newspapers and the internet) and especially the invaluable Algeria-Watch newsletters and website (https://algeria-watch.org/) since 1997. When I have used them as sources, this is noted in footnotes.

Back in 1992, Jill Knight[1] in Bangor had asked me to become the Algeria coordinator for Amnesty, taught me how to do the job and introduced me to the staff at the two Amnesty offices in London. At the International Secretariat, I learned so much from Donatella Roveda, Philip Luther and their research team who worked on human rights in Algeria for years. At the AIUK office, I helped on government matters – the Foreign Office in particular.

I have to thank many Amnesty members from around Britain, including Franki Gray and Sir Geoffrey Chandler[2] (heading the Business Group) and I must also acknowledge how I was welcomed to Parliament and introduced to many MPs and peers by Lord Avebury (Eric Lubbock),[3] an indefatigable fighter for human rights. The Head of UNA and three of us from AI, the Refugee Council and Freedom from Torture[4] met the Secretary of State and others in the Foreign Office before they visited Algeria.

The Country Coordinator for AI France, Monique Delboy, put me up and looked after me during visits I made to Paris; she had many invaluable French and Algerian contacts to whom I was introduced. I was also much assisted in Paris by Nassera Dutour and the mass of literature she gave me. I learned from other Country Coordinators who came from the Netherlands, Spain, Italy, Canada, the USA and elsewhere.

In North Wales, I received particular help and encouragement from Kevin Gill, who read more than one manuscript. I was also helped by Algerians and others from the Middle East, including

---

1   Died in 2018.
2   Died in 2011.
3   Died in 2016.
4   In the 1990s, this was called the Medical Foundation for the Care of Victims of Torture.

Abdel Futyan,[5] Omar Legrini and Bargas Hatem. I must also thank Amnesty members Maggie Towse and Gill Barnett for their help.

I thank all these and many others who assisted and encouraged me. In addition, I must thank my wife, Nellie, for being so patient during what seems years of my sitting upstairs in front of a screen.

---

5   Died in January 2019.

.

ABBREVIATIONS AND GLOSSARY

(Where the term is used only once or twice in the text, it is explained there.)

AI	Amnesty International.
AIS *Armée Islamique du Salut*	Islamic Salvation Army. Armed branch of *FIS*.
AIUK	Amnesty International UK. Section of AI.
ALN *Armée de libération nationale*	National Liberation Army that fought the War of Independence.
Al Qaida au pays du Maghreb islamique (AQMI)	*Al Qaida* in the Islamic Maghreb.
ANH	*Algeria News Highlights* Algeria. A two-monthly newsletter I compiled for British and international AI groups and for individuals from January 1994 until December 2004.
ANP *Armée nationale populaire*	People's National Army: the present-day army, descendant of the *ALN*.

AQMI/AQIM *Organisation d'Al-Qaida au pays du Maghreb islamique*	Al Qaida in the Islamic Maghreb.
AW	Algeria-Watch campaigns for human rights in Algeria, downloading thousands of articles from Algerian newspapers and elsewhere in French, German and English. It also produces its own reports and distributes this mass of material to its readers on its website (https://algeria-watch.org). It has been an invaluable source of material for this book.
Berbers	The peoples inhabiting North Africa since before the 7th century Arab conquest of the region, who have their own languages and customs.
Bidonvilles	Shanty towns.
CFDA	*Collectif des familles de disparu(e)s en Algérie:* Action Group of Families of the Disappeared, based in Paris.
DRS	*Direction des renseignments et de la sécurité:* Department of Intelligence and Security.
FFS	*Front des forces socialistes:* Socialist Forces Front, primarily Kabylia-based.
FIS	*Front islamique du salut:* Islamic party that would have won elections in 1992.
FLN	*Front de libération national:* National Liberation Front.
GIA *Groupe(s) islamique armé(s)*	Armed Islamic Group(s).
GPRA *Gouvernement Provisoire de la République d'Algérienne*	Provisional Government of the Algerian Republic.
GSPC	*Groupe salafiste pour la prédication et le combat:* Salafist Group for Preaching and Combat
IMF	International Monetary Fund
IS	The group that named itself 'Islamic State' or 'Daesh' in June 2014; it follows an Islamic fundamentalist and Wahabi doctrine of Sunni Islam.

Jihad	Means effort or struggle but routinely translated as 'holy war'.
LADDH Ligue algérienne pour la défense des droits de l'homme	League for the Defence of Human Rights. A significant HRs group.
LADH	*Ligue Algérienne des droits de l'homme:* Algerian League for Human Rights
MAOL	*Mouvement algérien des officiers libres: Algerian Movement of Free Officers.* A group of dissident Algerian officers based in Europe.
Maghreb (or Maghrib)	The western part of North Africa from Mauritania to Libya.
MEP	Member of European Parliament.
Mujahideen	Islamists engaged in *jihad* ('war'). Literally, *jihad* means striving or struggling to conform with God's guidance.
OAS	*Organisation de l'armée secréte:* Secret Army Organisation formed in early 1961 by French army deserters to try, by any means possible, to ensure that Algeria remained French.
OPEC	Organization of Petroleum Exporting Countries.
Pieds noirs	French and people of other nationalities who had come, since 1830, to settle in Algeria. The origin of the name is unknown.
le pouvoir	Literally means 'power'. The term refers to generals and those who run the country.
RCD	*Rassemblement pour la culture et la démocratie:* Rally for Culture and Democracy.
RND	*Rassemblement national démocratique:* National Democratic Rally.
Shari'a	Islamic law.
SM Sécurité militaire	Military Security. The precursor of the DRS: the name may still be used.
SOS disparus	Nassera's office in Algeria for the disappeared.

UGTA   *Union générale des travailleurs algériens:* Algerian Workers' General Union – trade union related to the *FLN*, it is the country's largest and most influential trade union.

Wali   One in authority; maybe the governor of a *wilaya*.

WB   World Bank.

Wilaya   Administrative region of Algeria, analogous to the French *département* or, in England, to a county.

MAP OF ALGERIA

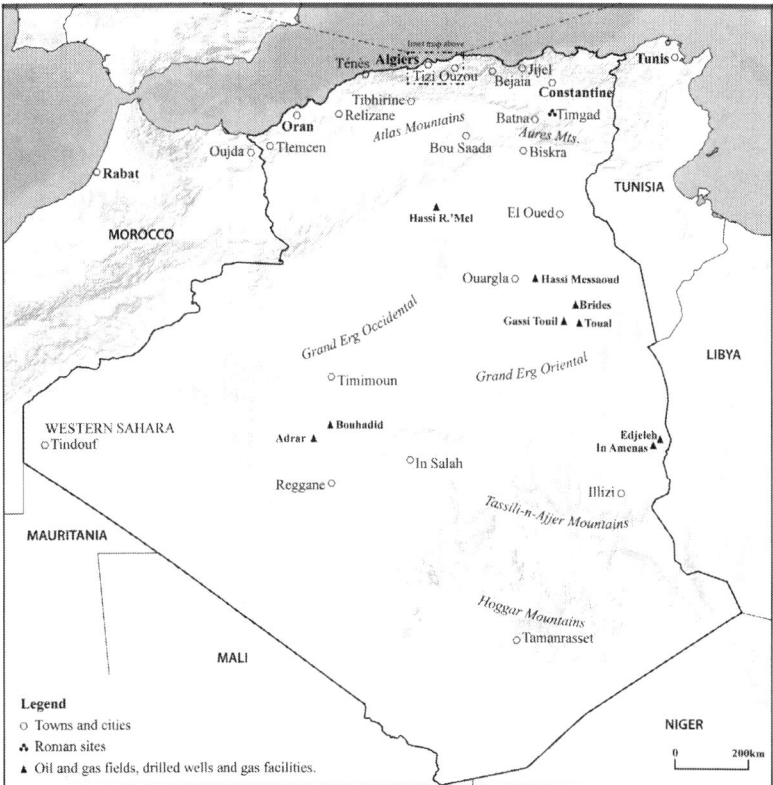

INTRODUCTION

I have followed the tragic fate of this resource-rich and beautiful country, and its generous and hospitable people, since its wild hopes for the future at the time of independence, until the present day. I write as a first-hand witness to the turbulent end of the War of Independence in 1962[1] and the extraordinary events following that day. I arrived in Algiers in January to work as a geologist in the oil and gas business. In the 1980s, I carried out work for the Algerian petroleum company Sonatrach, and then – for eighteen years (1994-2012) – at the most violent time of massacres and enforced disappearances of civilians, and the years following, I worked on human rights concerns for Amnesty International (AI) and an Algerian mother whose son 'disappeared'.

International news is selective and there are today too few investigative journalists. What is nowadays called 'breaking news' concentrates on the number of casualties and maybe on the terrible effect of a moment's killings on the relatives who are

---

[1]   The French never referred to what was going on in Algiers in 1962 as a war but to *les évènements* ('the events').

left to grieve completely unexpected deaths. A reporter stands in a bombed street and tries to answer impossible questions. After a day or two, interest moves to another catastrophe, other bombings, other communities shattered by bombs, 'terrorists'[2] or natural events. It can take years, or even decades, of investigative research and reporting to get close to the truth of what actually happened in many of these conflicts and – more importantly – to answer the question, why did they happen? This book will demonstrate the difficulty of arriving at the truth of what has happened, and continues to happen, in Algeria since 1962. At the same time, it may illustrate more clearly, in post-colonial history in much of the Middle East, North and West Africa and elsewhere, the dominant role of the military, the dependence on brutal secret services and the widespread corruption and abuse of power as well as the unending foreign interference of world powers in the internal affairs of supposedly independent countries.

My professional life began in Libya in 1956 with a small Texan company. There I learned, during four years 'on the job', predominantly in the Sahara, south of Sirte,[3] to understand rocks, so beautifully preserved there, to be a petroleum geologist and how to live and work in the desert. In Algeria later I had the good fortune, after being almost totally confined in 1962 to Algiers because of the dangers within the city and outside it, and having been evacuated to Paris for a year, to work in and to travel through considerable parts of the country.

Algiers in January 1962 was still a French city, and its centre a very beautiful one. It was called by some *Alger la blanche:* from the sea especially, the whitewashed buildings gave the impression of a glistening white city, climbing up the steep hills from the port.

---

2   *Terrorist* and *terrorism* are words that often seem to be used only for our enemies in war or other confrontations, are difficult to define, and the media do not use the terms for our own troops or civilians. I have tried, throughout this book, to put the words in inverted commas ('terrorist' or 'terrorism') and not to write terrorism or terrorist except in a quote.
3   Sirte became well known as Gaddafi's hometown; he was killed close to Sirte in 2011 during what has become known as the 'Arab Spring'.

Work on rigs took me with considerable frequency to the Sahara: mostly to the southeast of Hassi Messaoud, to and from which I flew innumerable times, once or twice in the most hazardous conditions. Hassi Messaoud, a town which had developed where the French had found vast oil deposits in 1956, was immediately recognisable from a great distance due to the flaring of gas which continually took place there.[4] At that time, Messaoud was just a base for the oil and gas business: now it is a very large town.

The rigs where I worked were a few hours' drive from Hassi Messaoud (Toual, Brides and others – see map[5]). One was in stony desert, several others in the sands of the immense Erg Oriental, which extend over an area of 600 by 200 kms. Rigs and the associated trailer/camps there were mostly sited among most beautiful sand dunes, proving early on that sand was not necessarily an impediment to extracting oil and gas. On one occasion, after heavy rain,[6] the surface of the dunes was so hard that it felt almost like concrete and could be driven over – if you could face the dangerously steep slopes.[7]

In September 1964, it was road or track all the way from Messaoud to Bouhadid, an exploration well near Adrar, far south in the Sahara. We passed through the unspoiled Sahara and desert oasis of Timimoun, of red-mud buildings, said to be

4   It is normal that gas is recovered together with oil, and if there is insufficient to produce economically, it is flared. I gave a talk about AI work in Algeria in the late 1990s, and two Algerians who had worked with Sonatrach told me that Hassi Messaoud gas was still flared at that time.
5   https://en.wikipedia.org/wiki/Devil%27s_Cigarette_Lighter. Gassi Touil caught fire in November 1961 and was extinguished six months later, just before I started working nearby at Brides. There was a 450-800 ft pillar of fire.
6   This was probably not as infrequent as thought by those unacquainted with deserts and, further north in the semi-desert area of northern Algeria, could cause considerable loss of life among villagers. The rain, although very heavy, would be local.
7   When I was in Libya there were a number of fatal accidents from careless and/ or fast driving and also in sand dunes, where the leeward (steep) side of dunes is particularly dangerous. One accident occurred by driving into an almost vertical 'cliff' face which the driver had probably not seen because of the bright sunlight and lack of shadow. I arrived in Libya at the very start of oil exploration there and hence there were no tracks from vehicles at all. A clean, pristine desert. I was most fortunate.

the place of imprisonment – house arrest – of Ahmed Ben Bella after he was removed from the presidency in 1965. The French Foreign Legion was alive and well in Adrar: this was no doubt because the town was only some 100 km north of Reggane where the French notoriously carried out four nuclear tests: the earliest on 13 February 1960.[8] The exploration well where I worked found a very significant amount of gas, which was regarded as of no interest at the time, but in the mid 1990s, when the price of gas had risen greatly, the area was taken up by BP, in conjunction with Norway's Statoil and the Algerian Sonatrach, to produce the gas; by the year 2006, when production started, this became a highly profitable venture.

Some of us took every opportunity after Independence day and in 1963-5 to travel outside Algiers[9] through villages close to the city, and especially to visit the beautiful Kabyle Mountains east of and not far from Algiers, and occasionally we travelled away for (long) weekends to this and neighbouring areas. This allowed us to drive along the coastal roads west from Algiers to Ténès and the small port of Tipasa with its extraordinary Roman remains. Later, we could travel east along a most beautiful road to Bougie (now Bejaia) and Jijel, up to the remarkable inland city of Constantine and the wonderful remains of the Roman city at Timgad. We went over the Atlas Mountains to the lovely oasis of Bou Saada more than once. East of this, and southwards from Batna, we passed through beautiful scenery completely disfigured by the sight of farmhouses and other houses gutted during the recent War of Independence. Then on to Biskra and the unique desert oasis of El Oued within the mighty sand dunes of the Eastern Erg. The white buildings glistened in the bright Saharan sunlight, and many were topped by little cupolas. Within the oasis, we could find a geological curiosity used as building stone: *roses de sable* (rock roses), formed by the evaporation of gypsum

---

8   Nuclear testing was not a matter of concern when I worked there in 1964-5.
9   It is likely that massacres took place in September 1997 in one or more of the villages that we visited outside Algiers. They would have greatly changed since 1965.

to form crystals shaped like rose petals – collectors' items. A somewhat lighthearted geological expedition in February 1965 took us down the oil fields on the east boundary of Algeria and then into the foothills of the Tassili Mountains at what was then Fort Polignac (now Illizi) and southwards. It must have been one of these days that we saw one of those wonders of nature: tiny fish swimming in a desolate desert pool. It would have been wonderful to travel further west to the extraordinary Hoggar Mountains and the marvellous cave paintings there, 5,000 to 8,000 years old. Now it is impossible due to the danger of kidnapping, which I shall describe later in this account.

One day, Algeria will be the country in North Africa that everybody will want to visit; Tunisia and Morocco may have all sorts of attractions, but Algeria has these and more – beaches, a beautiful coastline, the splendid Atlas Mountains and the Sahara Desert, with all its variety of terrain, mountains and dunes, colours and peoples. It is a wonderful and surprising country, and those people who are described in the following pages – dealing out executions, torture and mayhem – are not to be confused with the gentle, hospitable peoples of so much of the country.[10]

Two decades after I had first worked there, I visited Algiers in the late 1980s. The Algerian national oil and gas company, Sonatrach, funded by the World Bank, had opened a bidding process to produce a comprehensive assessment of the prospects of finding new oil and gas in the Algerian Sahara. The company for which I worked was awarded the project and as a result I and a colleague visited Sonatrach in Algiers several times during its compilation in the 1980s. The last time that we visited was in 1988, a critical year in Algeria's history. It was only much later that I could really understand how successful the project had been: it was at least in part as a result of this work that so much oil and gas was discovered in the Algerian Sahara in the 1990s and later.

---

10   A woman academic from Bangor University told me that she was treated appallingly by men when she visited Algiers University to give a lecture in, I think, the 1980s.

I have spent many years since 1994 studying Algeria and I have read much, mostly in French, which has been, over the years, the major language for writers on the subject.[11] I have been astonished by what I have learned: I can now understand something of what was going on. But still I do not understand fully some fairly basic events that impinged on us in 1962. Algeria has taught me how difficult it is to establish the truth: all sorts of people believe that they can say what happened, but…

It was the result of living in Algiers in the early 1960s – and in other countries where I learned of gross violations of human rights – that I really became aware of, and concerned about, human rights. In the late 1980s, I had joined the local AI group[12] in Colwyn Bay and worked on human rights violations which had been perpetrated in Syria[13] and Bolivia. By January 1994, the situation in Algeria had become of the greatest concern to Amnesty, and because of my previous experience in the country, I was asked to take on the task, as a volunteer, of what was called UK Country Coordinator Algeria. I shall describe this work in some detail; it became more than a full-time job for eleven years. Since that time I have continued to follow what is going

---

11   In recent years, Arabic has become important.

12   AI was founded in London in 1961, following the publication of the article *The Forgotten Prisoners* in the *Observer*, 28 May 1961 by the lawyer Peter Benenson. This article was published after Benenson had read about two Portuguese students who had been sentenced to seven years of imprisonment having allegedly 'drunk a toast to liberty'. Realising that this type of incident was happening in only too many countries, the article was published in the *Observer*, and reprinted in a large number of international newspapers to bring readers' attention to it, and to mobilise public opinion about those 'imprisoned, tortured or executed because their opinions or religion are unacceptable to the government.'

13   The work on Syria was a real eye-opener for me. The father of the present (2016) president, Hafez al-Assad (President 1971-2000), perpetrated the most vile human rights abuses in his prisons, killed 10,000 to 40,000 people in Hama in 1982 following an uprising there and was responsible for much else. This was well known, but the British government, which has been a strident voice since the 'Arab Spring' in 2011 in condemning Bashar al-Assad, did nothing from the early 1970s until now. The desk staff in the Foreign Office knew well what was going on in Algeria in the 1990s, just as those on the Syrian desk would have known about Syria: they did things 'quietly', they said, not using foghorn methods which, they suggested, AI was doing – which was quite true; we wanted as many people as possible to know what was going on.

on, on an almost daily basis, and to read many accounts to try and understand what has happened, how and why, in this sad, extraordinary and fascinating country.[14]

Whether looking at what has become known as 9/11, Algeria, or other 'terrorist' attacks, the press and television ask who? and what?, but it seems that the basic question is always: WHY? This is the reason that I have gone into the historical background of Algeria in this account: it helps to understand why these things happen, and to even approach understanding why man does such appalling things to his fellow men (it usually is men who do these things, but not always). This account is an example of the dreadful practices that go on in many countries of the world, some almost unknown. Algeria is not alone.

This book is not a dispassionate history of Algeria: I am neither a historian nor an academic. It is my personal attempt to give the flavour of what, almost unreported in Britain since the late 1990s, can happen in a country where the military are in control, where there is no rule of law, where there is no justice, where – in a resource-rich country – so many of the young, and others, have no hope for the future, except to try and emigrate to Europe.[15] Today we live in a world of instant news; reporters move on from one crisis to another, but it can sometimes take years, or even decades, of investigative research and reporting to get close to the truth of what has actually been going on. This book will demonstrate the difficulty of arriving at the truth in one country: Algeria. It is an attempt to unravel the complex issues that have caused so much suffering to so many and which still remain shrouded under a cloak of deception and misinformation. Algeria is by no means the only country where, following a colonial history, the military has a dominant role, there is a brutal secret service, widespread corruption and abuse of power.

---

14   I collected a large number of newspaper and magazine cuttings (British and others) until I was sufficiently competent to use a computer and find articles on the internet. When we moved house in 2010, I binned the cuttings, thinking I had no use for them – hence little reference to Robert Fisk and the writing of others.

15   Among those whom David Cameron, the UK Prime Minister at the time in late 2015, described as a 'swarm'.

'The first duty of government is to protect its people.'

'Il y a deux histoires: l'histoire officielle,
menteuse, puis l'histoire secrète, où sont
les véritables causes des événements.'

*('There are two histories: the official lying history and then
the secret history, where one finds the real causes of events.')*

1

LIFE IN FRENCH ALGERIA DURING
THE VIOLENT APPROACH TO INDEPENDENCE

Bodies lying in pools of blood in the streets of Algiers all day, buildings destroyed by bombs and fire, much of the city a complete no-go area for one or other of two communities, a total curfew from early evening to early morning – and despite this, no feeling of either law or order.[1] Rumour replaced information: newspapers and magazines were censored. There was no possibility of travelling many kilometres outside it, and for weeks, at the hottest time of the year in 1962, hundreds of thousands of people sought to leave the country.

I arrived in Algiers on Friday, 19 January, 1962, coming from Bolivia and the Amazon rainforest of the Andes foothills, where I had worked in the rivers as a geologist. I was royally welcomed in Algiers, the French enquiring why I had come – "because we are all leaving." The port and centre of Algiers was French, of handsome stone buildings and *boulevards;* narrow streets, steep

---

1   When I first arrived, there was a young French armed guard outside each bank. Soon they were no longer there since their arms had been stolen.

stone steps and passageways. A main square, soon to be known as the *Place des Martyrs* on account of a mortar attack which killed more than a hundred Algerian civilians, separated this part of the city clearly from the Turkish *casbah* and from less salubrious areas, where most of the Muslim population, and many of the *pieds noirs*,[2] lived. Elsewhere, the boundary was much less clear.

It was in Algiers that I began to learn directly about the darker side of life, about the dreadful things that men can do to others – but also about the resilience of those who try to bring about a better world. I had been assigned to work there for *CPA*,[3] the *Compagnie des Pétroles d'Algérie*, a subsidiary of Royal Dutch Shell. The *CPA* office was located not far from the city centre: it was about a kilometre to the main post office, which was situated at the beginning of what was then *la rue d'Isly*,[4] perhaps the most prestigious shopping street in the city at that time. This distance gave us a little exercise while walking to lunch and back by a variety of routes; it would also give us what was at first the traumatic experience of seeing bodies lying in pools of blood on the pavements; these were Muslims killed by *OAS*[5] sharpshooters – very sharp shooters in passing cars. The bodies would lie there all day and were collected at night during the curfew; the main road in front of the university library seemed to be a particular spot for these assassinations. This was where, on going into a tiny newsagent/tobacconist, a typical French *tabac*, an Algerian at the door – no more than three metres away from me – was

---

2   French and people of other nationalities who had come, since 1830, to settle in Algeria. The origin of the name is unknown.

3   *CPA* was one of four large companies searching for oil and gas in Algeria in 1962. (The other three were all 100% French.) It was a subsidiary of Royal Dutch Shell and the head office was in The Hague. It employed graduate international staff – like myself – French nationals, *pieds* noirs and Algerian Muslims, particularly in jobs in the laboratories, drawing office, secretarial work and suchlike. I quickly learned of French habits, such as shaking hands with all I met in the office every day, but never to offer my hand a second time.

4   Now *la rue Ben M'hidi Larbi*.

5   *OAS, L'Organisation de l'armée secrète*, Secret Army Organisation, formed in early 1961 by French army deserters and settlers to try, by any means possible, to ensure that Algeria remained French.

instantaneously shot dead: one very accurate and not loud shot; a phone call to the police, but the *buraliste* (the man who runs a *tabac* on behalf of the state) did not expect to see anyone.

Until independence on 5 July, and for some short time thereafter, Algiers was a divided city: those who lived in the European area did not go into the Muslim area and *vice versa*. Perhaps it was something innate that prevented us straying into Muslim areas.[6] Often, there was not much reason to go into the city since blinds of shops would be down. There were other days when the latest events, or rumours, had sent the population (many, no doubt, in a state of panic) to the shops for food, and at times there remained literally nothing on most of the shelves. There was a curfew every day from 2000 hrs until morning, which became a natural part of life. There were splendid beaches but, in view of what had happened on them, we spent a hot summer with perhaps a single visit to a single one. In Algeria as a whole, it has been reported[7] that in the first six weeks of 1962 alone there were 1,067 attacks causing 800 deaths and 1,480 injuries. In Algiers itself, the Muslim population was carefully and strictly controlled by their own community so that the French army would not intervene; and Muslims did indeed not respond – except on one day when many Europeans were killed by shots from speeding cars. The gunshots that we could hear on so many other occasions must have been primarily from the *OAS,* and except when they came out in force against a general strike or after major violence,[8] we never saw French soldiers on the street. Individuals carrying arms outside banks and public buildings when I arrived had their equipment taken from them

---

6   Although on one occasion, a colleague and I – driving around to occupy our time and to learn something about the city – arrived in an area surrounded by tall blocks of flats quite clearly occupied by Algerian families. We left quickly. I had no car – there was little one could do with it so I was kindly given lifts to the office and the Shell Club – just about our only destinations. I could also take a bus down to the city, but it became increasingly irregular and there were many days when there was a strike or other reasons why there would be no buses running.

7   These figures are from Lagarde, Dominique (collaborators: Akram Belkaid and Benjamin Stora), 2011 p 73. *Algérie: La désillusion. L'Express.*

8   When the area would be closed off.

by the *OAS,* so that after a while no more 'guards', and hence no more French soldiers, were to be seen.

On 19 March, an agreement, the *accords d'Evian,* had been reached between the French and the *GPRA,* the Provisional Government of Algeria, led by BenYoussef Ben Khedda, and a ceasefire was proclaimed. Within Algeria, the result was that the level of *OAS* violence increased greatly; we did not know it but on 21 March, the *OAS* announced that the French forces in Algeria were now regarded 'as occupation troops'.[9] On 26 March, I noted in my diary: *Went to work, left at 10.30. Demonstration to march on Bab-el-Oued*[10] *– shot down. Complete curfew on town. Alive with helicopters,*[11] and again on the next day: *Went to work, left at 09.30. General Strike.*[12] The strike and march to Bab-el-Oued had been called by the *OAS* but, following machine-gunning from a window and the riposte of French soldiers, the day ended with some sixty deaths and nearly 200 wounded in the rue d'Isly shopping street.[13] There was one day when there was shooting in several parts of the city, only too audible from the flat – it must have been a weekend or a strike day. We were told that it was the one day when the Muslim population had not been able to control all its elements, and young men – apparently starting from a number of parts of the Muslim city – raced through the streets of the European parts of the city, shooting those on the streets. It did not happen again.[14] Mostly the shooting and noise

---

9   Stora 1995 p 77.
10   According to Groussard (1972, p 93), a minimum of 140 *pieds noirs* were killed in Bab-el-Oued. It was a poor, crowded part of the city, inhabited only by Europeans at the time; my diary states on 23 March: *battle of Bab el-Oued.* The 'Battle of Bab el-Oued' was between French *gendarmes* and the *OAS.*
11   This is somewhat inscrutable: the march was ended by live shooting taking place.
12   My diary tells little of life in Algiers; it is an undistinguished set of notes, mostly of the work that I did, days when we couldn't go to work and dates when colleagues and families departed Algiers. At the time, I did not wish to record the violence that was going on.
13   Groussard (1972, p 93) Stora wrote that Bab-el-Oued was in the hands of 'partisans of French Algeria'.
14   Groussard (p 96, 103) states that hundreds of Europeans were murdered by what were called *les incontrolés*; Groussard – who was a fervent supporter of the *OAS* – believes that the *FLN* was behind these.

were at night – during the curfew, of course; I have a diary note that says, on 23 March: *Shots more or less continuous from 11 at night. Curfew.*[15] *No electricity after midnight.*

On 2 April, my diary notes that I saw French troops searching the city centre area of the high-class Aletti Hotel, close to the port. The departure *en masse* of *pieds noirs* and others to France commenced in April. On 10 April, the diary records: *Worked till 07.30.*[16] *No buses.*[17] *Walked to Hydra. Telephone communications at Hydra blown up.* In order to live with such a situation, we went to the office or, when that was not possible, worked at home and convinced ourselves that we were living a normal life. General Raoul Salan, the leader of the *OAS*, was arrested on 20 April (in an apartment block very close to the office), judged and sentenced to life imprisonment.

On 7 June, as part of an *OAS* 'scorched earth' policy, the university library, with 300,000 books, went up in flames, which burned fiercely all day and continued for another couple of days.[18] And that same afternoon, a primary school across the road from the office was blown up and burned down: an enormous log landed on a first-floor balcony of the office. The *OAS* wanted to leave nothing of value to an independent Algeria. The Air France office had been one of the first buildings to be destroyed: this was done to try and prevent *pieds noirs* from leaving the country; it was not rebuilt – it could not have been. This meant that, to the hell and tragedy of leaving a country that had been their home, some for generations, was added the hell of what could be several days, in a seething mass of maybe thousands, under the scorching

---

15 In fact, there was a curfew every night and also at times a curfew during the day, when nobody was permitted to travel to the city.

16 I cannot remember whether we started work at 06.30 or 07.00 but we worked very long hours – until 1800 hrs, including Saturday mornings. Lunch breaks were very French; I recollect three hours long. Hydra is high above Algiers Port – perhaps 300 m (1,000 ft); buses had not operated for some weeks and my diary notes that they restarted on 20 April, with Arab staff.

17 I often took the bus until it did not run for some weeks. Muslim drivers replaced *pieds noirs* who had presumably departed.

18 It was a terrible conflagration and flames quickly rose high in the sky. I happened to be in front of the library when the first bomb exploded.

sun of May and June, trying to get out of the country by any means. From the end of May, 8,000 to 10,000 per day left the country with just their most precious possessions in a suitcase or two: the port and airport of Algiers were a mass of humanity and struggle. Most had to abandon their cars beside the roadside on the way to the airport, alongside hundreds of others – and then leave from the port or airport, where thousands of people waited in near-riotous conditions. Many had never even been to France, were not welcomed, and to this day live miserable lives there.

Did we who lived there know what was going on? The answer is NO. We knew remarkably little: there would be 'facts', such as accounts and estimates of people killed and injured and buildings bombed. There would be accounts of the *OAS*, but almost nothing to allow one to really understand what was happening – newspapers were often censored and some banned by the French authorities, and those which were available in Algiers gave their own slant on things.[19] Radio was the primary source of news and it seems clear that news from France was likely to have been only what the French wished to transmit. There was news from London transmitted by the BBC World Service and this should probably have been the most reliable, but I don't remember it giving much explanation of what was happening. It was said that foreign reporters in Algiers would install themselves in the bar of the four-star Hotel Aletti[20] near the port, and await news from local people. In such a situation, one could well ask what the locals really knew – Algiers was continually awash with rumours such as "the water has been poisoned"... Surely what was passed on was what somebody wished to pass on, and it is likely that many foreign reporters would not have had the background or the knowledge to sift well what they heard.

Certain communications arrived only too frequently: tracts showing photographs of people who had been most horrifically

---

19 *Le Monde,* for example, was hardly ever available. *L'Aurore,* fervently right wing and supporting the *pieds noirs,* was nearly always on sale. I myself had arrived in Algiers with no French, but there were British, Dutch, Swiss and, of course, French, who had been there some years and who would have been able to enlighten a new arrival had they known what was going on.

20 Now the *Es Safir.*

tortured and killed, which was presumably propaganda from the *OAS*, were dropped into one's letterbox – which was on the ground floor of a very large block of flats, accessible to all. Above all, the Europeans – and no doubt the whole population of Algiers – lived on rumours, many of the most unbelievable type, but in those days I was very naive. Looking back, it is likely that it was impossible to know what was happening, since the most improbable and conflicting rumours emanated from all sides.[21]

On 18 June, the *FLN* (*Front de Libération*)[22] and *OAS* signed a ceasefire in Algiers but this was rejected in Oran, the only Algerian city with a European majority. Six banks were attacked and cleaned out: the *OAS* was preparing its departure by sea, with arms and large sums of money. *Pieds noirs* and others waited for the ferry or plane to France in total disorder: they just had to flee this country, 'to which they would remain attached with all their being but which had become a hell.'[23]

A referendum in both Algeria and France on 1 July 1962 confirmed Algerian independence: 99.72% voted yes and more than 91% of those eligible voted. General de Gaulle recognised Algeria as independent on 3 July and Algeria celebrated on 5 July.

VIOLENCE AND WAR IN FRENCH ALGERIA (1830-1962)

What was the background to the violence going on in Algiers since I arrived? It was, of course, the end of the War of Independence[24] between the French and Algerians. I shall touch very rapidly on

---

21 It is interesting to conjecture that in so many areas of violence, the earliest news stories will be remembered by the general public, without any evidence that these are reporting the truth of what was happening. When later and more reliable accounts are in the news, many may only remember what they first heard.
22 The *FLN* had organised an insurrection on 1 November 1954 that led to the War of Independence.
23 Stora 1995 p 80.
24 It is only recently that the French have recognised that it was a war. In 1962, it was referred to by the French as *les* évènements. Quite recently, I noticed that the names of local people killed in Algeria have been added to some war memorials in France.

the colonial years from 1830[25] and the War of Independence (1954-62), doing so in a very summarised fashion.[26]

France took the best land after it invaded in 1830, while the Arab peasant was left with, on average, no more than three hectares of poor land, whether this was sufficient to live on or not. The adversary, said General Bugeaud, the Governor General, "had to be hunted, tracked down and destroyed."[27] A thousand men were asphyxiated in a cave and some women were auctioned to the troops like animals.[28] By 1849, Algeria had lost a quarter of its population, and the north of the country had become three *départements* of France.

Moving on to the 20th century, the First World War was of the greatest significance to Algeria:[29] Algerian peasants and others were requisitioned to go to France to work in the mines and agriculture and, for the first time, became involved in politics, influenced by the Russian Revolution and Woodrow Wilson's 1917 proclamation of the rights of peoples to independence. *Pieds noirs* met Algerian Muslims and nearly 50,000 from the two communities died on the battlefields. After the war, land in Algeria became more concentrated in the hands of major landowners. The old tribal society broke down and migration to shanty towns (*bidonvilles)* in the towns followed. Immigrants in France formed the first Algerian political party and called unsuccessfully for Algerian independence.

On the very last day of World War II, cessation of hostilities in Europe – 8 May 1945 – there was the first spontaneous uprising in eastern Algeria. This rapidly escalated and Muslims attacked Europeans in a number of towns: 110 Europeans were killed. A massacre followed which led to the deaths of at least 15,000 Muslims. General Duval, who was responsible, said: "I have given you ten years of peace. But you mustn't delude yourselves. Everything has to change in Algeria."[30] He was remarkably perceptive, but the

---

25 Algeria became an integral part of France (three departments) in 1848.
26 It has been the subject of more than a thousand books (Stora, 1995 p 3).
27 Stora, 1991 p 20.
28 Bennoune, 1998 p 40.
29 Stora, 1991, pp 44ff.
30 Stora, p 91.

drama was that practically nothing had changed when the War of Independence began on 1 November 1954. Peasant ways of life continued to be destroyed, and the Mayor of Algiers said the population living in *bidonvilles* multiplied twenty-five times to 125,000; these people had no future.

THE WAR FOR ALGERIAN INDEPENDENCE (1954-62)[31]

Algeria had not just been a French colony; it had been an integral part of France – three *départements,* in fact, since 1848. Between midnight and 0200 hrs on 1 November 1954, thirty coordinated attacks on towns announced the beginning of the War of Independence[32] during which hundreds of thousands were killed and maybe half the rural population displaced. Six French presidents were brought down and nearly two million French conscripts crossed the Mediterranean to engage in a bitter war. There are vast numbers of varied and contradictory views about the war, its background and outcome. Stora asked: 'Why had it been so bitter?'[33] After the climactic loss of French Indochina in May 1954, some of the generals who went to North Africa decided that under no account would Algeria be lost too.

The independence movement in Algeria was both socialist[34] and traditionally Islamic, and a nationalistic ideology gave rise to the notion of a nation 'guided' by a single party: the *FLN*. The *FLN* had one overriding goal: national independence. Abdane Ramdane, who had spearheaded the movement for political leadership within the *FLN* over the military, was assassinated in 1957.[35] This murder is regarded by some as the foundational

---

31 Stora, 1991, p 109. I have followed Stora in this summary.
32 Stora, 1995, p 9.
33 Stora, 1995, p 3.
34 Following Nasser in Egypt and others.
35 December 1957. (Stora 1995 p 44. and Roberts 2003 p 47ff.) As early as mid-1956, *FLN* delegations were set up in world capitals and sought help, both material and political, from them. In October, a Moroccan plane was forced to land at Algiers Airport and Algerian leaders were imprisoned.

event which gave rise to military rule in Algeria.[36] Several other murders of leaders followed.

The so-called 'Battle of Algiers' in early 1957[37] was notorious for bombs placed by attractive young Muslim women in cafes and places where *pieds noirs* gathered, for the brutality of torture by the French[38] to break the 'rebellion', and for the 'disappearance' of thousands of Muslims. The French use of torture, which divided France, was said to have been quite general, and General Paris de Bollardière asked to be relieved from his post because of the methods used.[39]

A powerful Algerian army, the *armée des frontières,* had been built up in Morocco and Tunisia in the late 1950s, but this was cut off by the French, who built impenetrable electrified fences along both frontiers. Already, as early as 1958, the *FLN* was being assisted by other countries, including the UK and the USA, with supplies of armaments and other material, often through Morocco or Tunisia.[40] Late on in the War of Independence, many junior Algerian officers (called the *DAF*[41]) deserted from the French army to Boumediène's *armée des frontières*; some would become powerful generals in the 1990s.

In May 1958, a constitutional crisis in France led to General de Gaulle becoming President of France. After three days, he visited Algeria and was perhaps best remembered for his enigmatic response to the crowd: "*Je vous ai compris.*"[42] The *pieds noirs* assumed he meant them, but when later he spoke of 'self-determination', and other African countries became independent,

36 Laribi, 2007, p 21.
37 Stora, 1995, p 44ff.
38 The Italian classic film *The Battle of Algiers* displays only too realistically the French use of torture. It was banned from being shown in France for five years.
39 A Frenchman, a colleague in Algiers who had earlier been a conscript in the country during the war, later told me that Algerian Muslims used the same methods against the French in the War of Independence.
40 When working in Libya in the Sahara in 1958-59, low-flying unmarked planes would fly over us in a westerly direction. We were sure they were carrying armaments and material to help the *FLN*.
41 *DAF*: *Déserteurs de l'armée française.*
42 There have been thousands of words written about this phrase, but to whom was it addressed?

they became worried. When de Gaulle said on 11 April 1961 that 'decolonisation is in our interest', a parachute regiment occupied the main buildings in Algiers; the effect of de Gaulle's broadcast that evening denouncing "retired generals... with a limited and cursory know-how," heard by conscript soldiers on transistor radios, was electric, and the *putsch* failed. General Raoul Salan, the most decorated French general, who had earlier been Commander-in-Chief, had left Vietnam determined that Algeria would remain French. He deserted to lead the *OAS*, which practised the worst sort of crimes, and seemed to be supported by most *pieds noirs*.[43] Practically all Europeans in the cities, particularly those who were less well off, gave their enthusiastic support to the *OAS*,[44] joining in demonstrations such as days of *les concerts de casseroles* – a very noisy banging on saucepans to the rhythm of '*Algérie française*', three short and two long bangs.[45] Car horns in the city set up the same cacophony all day.[46] The fervour increased and Salan announced that by the end of 1961, he would have 100,000 armed and disciplined men. There was disappointment when de Gaulle escaped an attempt on his life.[47]

The French army had believed in early 1961 that it had won the military war against the *FLN*, but the *FLN* was by that time widely recognised and supported internationally.[48] It had come together sufficiently for negotiations with the French government to begin in France in 1960, and peace negotiations followed in Evian-les-Bains in March 1962.[49] Meanwhile, half of the rural population in Algeria had been displaced by the war, and a million men were unemployed.

---

43 Stora, 1995, p 60.

44 Stora, 1995, p 61.

45 This was particularly performed when de Gaulle's press conferences were broadcast on the radio.

46 I quickly became used to this when I arrived in Algiers and there was a short tunnel near the university where it seemed obligatory for drivers always to sound '*Algérie française*'.

47 This was by no means the only assassination attempt on de Gaulle.

48 Including the UK and the USA.

49 Stora, 1995, p 60f.

2

TWO MILITARY COUPS FOLLOW THE JOY OF INDEPENDENCE (1962 - 1988)

The War of Independence had destroyed French Algeria. What would replace it?

INDEPENDENCE DAY (5 JULY 1962)

For Algerians, Independence Day, 5 July 1962,[1] was an extraordinary day of the greatest joy.[2] They had won a victory over the French, they had the benefits of the riches of enormous deposits of oil and gas in the Sahara and they were free of

---

1   De Gaulle, following elections both in Algeria and France, had declared Algeria independent on 3 July, but official celebrations took place – as they have done since that time – on 5 July.

2   Except in Oran where, following what was assumed to have been a last *OAS* fusillade, more than eighty Algerians and twenty-five to forty-six French were killed, according to different sources. On 5 July, and on the days preceding, some 2,000 people – European and Algerian – had been kidnapped, executed or 'disappeared' (Ait Benali Boubekeir: *Du 19 Mar to 5 Jul 1962: une périlleuse transition*, Algeria-Watch 5 Jul 2010).

colonialism. They had enormous hopes and expectations of a better life and they would not have to remain in poverty. It was a wonderful, wonderful day. Everyone was in their best clothes, some young boys were dressed as *mujahideen* with wooden submachine guns (were they using real ones thirty years later?) and girls were dressed in the colours of the Algerian flag. I seemed to be the only European to watch the statue of the hated Marshal Bugeaud, who had from 1830 been accused of genocide, being manhandled down from its imposing pedestal in the main shopping street of Algiers. Large groups of women appeared in public for perhaps the first time ever. Life would never be the same again... I conversed with deliriously happy Algerians who were only too pleased to see me and welcome me to their country; I do not remember seeing other Europeans in what had been the French part of the city that day – perhaps in view of what occurred in Oran it was unwise to go there, and it remains etched in my memory. But, there was a very big dark cloud, and more than a cloud, and not just on the horizon, which none of them believed; they had thought it was 'French propaganda'. As is required on the first day of independence, new leaders appeared on the balcony of the Algiers Prefecture, but only some of them – where were the rest, the military leaders... all those others whom the crowd wished to see? How many Algerians realised that independence, with its promise of freedom, was about to give rise to military rule, whose yoke – much tightened in the early 1990s – they are still under fifty-seven years later? It transpired that 5 July 1962 would be a day the likes of which would never be seen again.

A BLOODY MILITARY COUP: BOUMEDIÈNE'S ARMY TAKES OVER

Life for those of us in Algiers now consisted of going down to the office in the mornings, doing our work in much easier conditions than in *OAS* times, sometimes visiting the 'Shell Club' in the afternoons and going back up again in the evenings. The big difference was that there were now so few of us expatriates; families had long departed. Those who went to Europe for the most part did not return, and we understood that the Shell head office in The Hague was informed that all was well. Those of us who were left, as I have mentioned, did start travelling at weekends outside Algiers and particularly to the east[3]. It was now thought that it would be safe to do so and we were not aware that an army from Tunisia/Morocco might be advancing into Algeria. But surely French radio[4] or newspapers, which we read when they were not censored – which was only too often – must have had reports of this?

One beautiful, sunny morning, which my diary tells me was 9 September, driving down to the office, we found that major road junctions were manned by very smart armed soldiers behind barricades with rifles at the ready: they gave every indication that their mission was very serious. Who were they? Why were they there, and what was going on? It seems curious to state that we had no idea, and the more I consider it, the odder it now seems that we really had no clue of what was occurring. Algiers, like the other *wilayas*[5] loyal to the *GPRA*, kept on holding out for elections.[6] Apparently, Boumediène's army had attacked *wilaya IV* (Algiers area) units on 29 August, resulting in many deaths: the people of Algiers came down into the streets shouting, "S*ept ans, ça suffit.*" ("Seven years, that's enough.") However, following a *Bureau politique*[7] order the next day to *wilayas I, II V and VI*[8] and to the army to march on Algiers, there were more than a

---

3   It had of course been unsafe to go before Independence Day.
4   Which, unlike newspapers, we could receive without difficulty. There is a comment on 4 September in my diary: *Ceasefire agreed between Ben Bella troops* (Wilayas I, II V and VI and local forces (III & IV), but it meant little to me.
5   Administrative region of Algeria, analogous to the French *département* or in English to county or province.
6   Elections originally announced for 5 December were 'delayed' (Stora 2001).
7   The military government formed by Ben Bella.
8   Those loyal to the *armée des frontières*; *wilaya IV* – the *Algérois,* the area around Algiers, and *wilaya V* – Kabylia – were still loyal to the *GPRA*.

thousand deaths in violent clashes in towns leading to the city.[9] We knew nothing of this.

The next day, 10 September, I went for the first time to the Algerian Sahara to work on rigs there – something I had been requesting almost since my arrival in January. Unlike probably every other oil company, Shell did not employ geologists on rig work, a curious decision as I trust I was able to demonstrate – in any case, from then on, I spent considerable periods of time back where I preferred to be: in the desert.[10]

Back up north, though, something much worse had been happening, of which we were also unaware at the time. Many Algerian Muslims (who have become known as *harkis*[11]) had cooperated with the French; some French officers had wanted desperately – and quite rightly in view of what followed – to help those who had worked for them to get to France, but de Gaulle forbade this and measures were taken to ensure that the order was followed. These officers stated that "*Nous avons perdu notre honneur avec la fin de cette guerre d'Algérie.*" ("With the ending of this war, we have lost our honour.")[12] For the officers, they were the faithful servants of France. For Algerian nationalists, they were absolute traitors. Thousands[13] were massacred, and not just massacred: Stora[14] writes that between 27 July and

9   Stora, 2001, pp 14-15, writes of a civil war. It is more generally considered that a civil war was averted; Roberts, 2003, p 115f explains, using Ireland as an example, that a civil war has often led to democracy, and argues that it is perhaps the fact that there was no civil war, just a splintering – but no break-up of the *FLN* – that Algeria was unable to develop along the path of democracy.

10   In Libya, in addition to carrying out what was regarded as real geological work – with a hammer and other equipment, working on rocks beautifully exposed at the surface – I had worked on rigs and learned how to tackle geology below the surface of the ground.

11   A derogatory and insulting term, meaning a traitor who places himself beyond society – Stora in *Reporters sans frontières* 1996 p 73; many of those who did escape to France live to this day in the most miserable conditions. The number of 263,000 was reported in this article. Roberts says, in a personal communication, that *les harkis* did not 'work' for the French; they fought and killed and, in plenty of cases, raped and tortured for them.

12   Stora, 1995, p 80.

13   57,000 according to the historian Charles-Robert Ageron (Stora *Reporters sans frontières* 1996 p 75) who writes that other sources suggest 100,000.

14   *Reporters sans frontières,* 1996, p 75.

mid-September 1962, dozens of *harkis* were dragged, dressed as women, noses, ears and lips cut, emasculated, buried alive in chalk or cement or burned alive by petrol; others in another village were crucified on doors. These were the pitiful after-effects of a terrible war. None of this did I learn at the time.

The kidnapping of Europeans at the time of independence was something else we did not know. But we came to learn about this only too intimately: on 11 September, a message was received at the rig where I had arrived the previous day to say that the senior manager of *CPA*, Jacques Follot, had gone missing. His body was found some days later but we never knew who killed him. It seemed to me that this was most likely a political assassination[15] since he was the senior manager left in *CPA*, a firm believer that Shell must stay in Algeria to show support for the new government, and on the same day we learned that a senior Michelin manager was also assassinated. So Shell in The Hague learned that everything had not been normal, and the Shell machine now started to move with increasing urgency.[16]

We were evacuated to Paris on 12 October 1962, to continue working on (and in) Algeria. Paris could not escape the bloody result of what had been going on in Algeria: a failed assassination attempt on de Gaulle in a Paris suburb on 22 August 1962[17] gave rise to my meeting when driving in the Bois de Boulogne some months later, a line of twenty black Citroen cars, nineteen with a de Gaulle look-alike.

We would remain almost exactly a year in Paris, returning on 18 October 1963. Presumably, the country would be peaceful, but no; we sat in Algiers Airport for three hours because there were demonstrations in the city. The so-called 'war of the sands' had just broken out with Morocco – who claimed a large part

---

15 Wim Goudswaard, a good colleague and friend, told me that there was speculation that Jacques Follot was killed, perhaps by an ex-employee of *CPA* with a grudge, in order to take his expensive Citroën. His body was found, Wim told me, in a ditch in a nearby suburb.

16 Did Shell not learn that the *armée des frontières* had been advancing into the country since 11 July?

17 De Gaulle was reported to have got out of the car and said, "What poor shots!"

of the Sahara. A truce and resolution was agreed at the end of the month, but there have been continuing disputes between Morocco and Algeria since that time. What else had happened in this ever-turbulent country during the year that we were absent?

After a war lasting seven and a half years which took the lives of hundreds of thousands of Algerians, and with the departure of some million Europeans, many of whom had effectively administered and managed the country – not to mention doctors, teachers, technicians, highly skilled workers and others – the situation in Algeria was desperate: more than 40% of the population was living in the most abject misery; the traditional peasant's life had been destroyed and the economy was wrecked.[18] Some 8,000 villages and hamlets had been destroyed, forests burned, mines had been laid on cultivated land and the country's livestock, especially of sheep, was almost decimated[19]. Following independence, more than 90,000 Algerians left for France between 1 September and mid-November 1962: France had hoped for movement in the opposite direction. But there was also a positive legacy from colonialism: modern cities and towns and all that goes with them – railways, roads and airports, huge oil and gas fields. We noticed evidence of Russian and Chinese presence in Algiers, perhaps providing expertise and support for the new government following the departure of the *pieds noirs,* as well as building up a relationship that would benefit them.

BEN BELLA BECOMES PRESIDENT (1963)

The entry of Boumediène's army into Algiers in September 1962 had allowed the *FLN bureau politique* to achieve its goals of taking power and of eliminating other opposition in a *coup d'état*. The single list of official candidates for elections received 90% of the vote, and

18   Stora, 2001, p 7ff.
19   Bennoune, p 89ff.

the socialist **Ahmed Ben Bella** became Head of Government. The *FLN* had become the *parti unique* (single party), with the army at the centre of power: the list of candidates for the National Assembly had been amputated so that there was a single list, elected, it was said, by 99% of voters on 30 September. The government now included five military in key posts – one of them Boumediène – but nobody from the army had appeared on the balcony on 5 July. All political parties other than the *FLN* were denounced: they demonstrated a division among the people, which must be united in the *parti unique*. There must be no political pluralism: Algeria had become a one-party state and remained so until 1988; the only legal opposition was the small vocal Communist party. The *coup* had been meticulously planned, all in any position were spied upon, and many who were unscrupulous individuals or simply opportunists gained prized situations, while those who had been true and loyal more often lost out. But the social situation was alarming with two million out of work and 2.6 million without resources, and so many qualified technicians, administrative staff and others had departed for Europe.[20]

Algeria followed Nasser's Egypt by opting for a form of socialism: *autogestion*, which meant worker or cooperative management, the running of businesses by the employees. This became the key theme to mobilise and transform Algeria: it was introduced 'from above' to a country that was neither materially nor politically ready for it.[21] The new Algeria was anti-imperialist and regarded as the leader, in the 1960s and '70s, of the Third World.[22] The sociologist Abdelkader Djeghloul said that 'this Algeria scarcely resembled that dreamed of by the first fighters in November 1954.'[23] Although the *FLN* had given the

---

20   There was an agreement with France that technical cooperation (*coopération technique*) would be provided. The registration number of my car in late 1963 became CT9.

21   Aggoun & Rivoire, 2005, p 49f

22   'Algiers was the mecca of revolutionary movements from the Third World who came to seek financial assistance, diplomatic help and ideological inspiration.' (Laddi *L'Orient Le Jour, 6 Jun* 2015).

23   Stora, 2001, p 19.

impression of disintegrating in the summer of 1962, it did not do so and was able to handle its bitter internal divisions without splitting, and so avoid civil war, which was very much on the cards. The *FLN* was not a political party 'in the proper sense of the word' but a 'political movement fighting a revolutionary war for nationalist purposes.'[24] The war it launched was based in the Algerian countryside, and it was these rural traditions that impinged upon the thinking of its leaders. On the positive side, it must be said that those who fought and died for the Algerian cause during the war (*chuhada* - martyrs) retained a special status, and a ministry looked after the welfare of their families.

THE SECOND COUP: BOUMEDIÈNE OUSTS BEN BELLA AND BECOMES PRESIDENT (1965)

Ben Bella had wanted to take action against Colonel Boumediène[25] but he did not dare.[26] Instead, he tried to reduce the influence of those behind Boumediène. In 1965, this led to an almost bloodless *coup d'état*: Ben Bella was arrested and not released for fifteen years, and Boumediène headed a Revolutionary Council which assumed all powers in June 1965, shortly after I left the country.

Boumediène, like Ben Bella, was the son of poor peasants: he was described as secretive, and an inflexible, austere ideologue,[27] but he succeeded in establishing a more broadly based regime representing all major factions of the wartime *FLN*. The regime was utterly ruthless in removing all opposition by means of the feared *Securité militaire* (*SM*).[28] More *chefs historiques* and

---

24   Roberts, 2003, p 40f.
25   Colonel was the highest rank in the army at the time.
26   Stora, 2001, p 31.
27   Stora, 2001, p 34f.
28   Sifaoui (2014, p 28) notes that the *SM* was formed during the War of Independence, well before Algeria became a nation state in 1962. The *SM* (from 1990, officially known as the *DRS*) has regarded itself as possessing a power 'superior' to the State.

leaders went into exile and/or were assassinated.[29] At least two attempts on Boumediène's life were unsuccessful and he came to be regarded as invincible.

Whereas agriculture was to be the basis of economic growth in an *FLN* programme agreed just before independence, and Ben Bella made this his first priority,[30] Boumediène concluded that the country must industrialise, and massive iron and steel complexes were built on the coast. There were big advances in healthcare and in education during the Boumediène regime;[31] Algeria's population tripled in thirty years after independence, and in 1984, the birth rate was 6.1 per woman: 60% of the population was less than twenty years old and schools rotated shifts of two hours per day. Expanding numbers of university graduates were looking for work in a contracting public sector, health services declined, infrastructure crumbled and the countryside became pauperised in favour of heavy industry.[32]

It was during this time that **corruption** networks, which were to become such a thorn in Algeria's back, were set up. "No contract for imports signed by a national enterprise is able to escape the payment of a commission" the Minister of Economy of the time said.[33] It became a means of obtaining power.

For the military bureaucracy who had taken power in 1965, **history** had to be **rewritten**. The role of the *maquis* in the interior of the country – who had done the fighting – must be re-

---

29   One of those was Mohamed Khider, who was assassinated in Madrid in January 1967 by the Algerian military security. The killer was later arrested and probably executed – this became the classic procedure, in order to leave no witnesses (Aggoun & Rivoire, p 59); a second was Belkacim Krim who was assassinated in Germany in October 1970 (Aggoun & Rivoire, p 61).

30   The agricultural programme was beset with bureaucratic problems and the destruction of the peasant way of life (Bennoune, p 97, 104ff). Boumediène had planned 1,000 'socialist villages', but this project was beset with problems of greed, the incompetence of political leaders and corruption.

31   At independence, only 10% of children of school age went to school; twenty years later, the number of teachers had multiplied twenty-seven times and girls made up 40% of school pupils and 25% of university graduates.

32   Entelis in Martinez, 2000, pp xi-xii.

33   Aggoun and Rivoire, 2005, p 66, from Mahfoud Bennoune and Ali el-Kenz *Le Hasard et l'Histoire* p 211. Boumèdiéne tolerated corruption since it allowed him to control those involved.

presented, as must certain episodes in history, and the *armée des frontières,* although its role was quite insignificant, must have an important place.[34] The terrible settling of scores when thousands were killed was deleted, as was any mention of the differing political views of Messali Hadj, Ferhat Abbas and the religious *ulema* (religious scholars and doctors of law), which were so significant in forming ideas about modern Algerian nationalism in the thirty years prior to the War of Independence. There had been no splits within the *FLN,* and the Algerians and those in power had been united since 1 November 1954.[35] A National Centre of Historic Studies (*CNEH*) was set up in 1974 to ensure that the 'correct' history was published.[36]

On 24 February 1971, it was announced that Boumediène had **nationalised the oil and gas industry** and that an agreement had been signed with France on 29 July 1965 which should take into consideration the reciprocal interests of the two countries;[37] he said that five years later, Algeria had followed the agreement and France had not.[38] For Boumediène and Algeria, this was a stroke of genius,[39] but for the French, who had dominated oil and gas exploration and production throughout Algeria, and were now afraid of another Cuba on their southern shore, it was a bombshell. A left-turn in Algerian politics had occurred, described by Boumediène as *la Révolution socialiste:*[40] this included the nationalisation of large agricultural estates and the establishment of a collective farm sector.

The Organization of Petroleum Exporting Countries[41] shocked the world by forcing a tripling of oil prices in 1973.

---

34 Stora, 2001, p 70.
35 Lahouari Addi: *L'écriture de l'Histoire et ses implications politiques en Algérie, Le Soir d'Algérie,* 28 Jun 2010.
36 Algeria is by no means unique in designing a 'correct' version of its history.
37 I was in Nigeria and I well remember how the oil and gas business was stirred up at the time.
38 Roberts, 2003, p 13ff, points out that it was unconstitutional.
39 Malti, 2010, p 61.
40 Entelis, in Martinez, 2000, pp xi-xii.
41 OPEC. Founded in 1960 by the Islamic Republic of Iran, Iraq, Kuwait, Saudi Arabia and Venezuela. Other countries joined later, including Algeria.

This was the trigger for a big increase in revenues from Algeria's oil and gas exports, which led to a disastrous Soviet-style industrialisation programme. Although the income was still not sufficient for the investments planned, it allowed Algeria to seek massive international loans, which were a noose about its neck until the big increase of petroleum prices in the early 21st century. The **oil price**, which has always been of such significance to Algeria's economy, had risen markedly in 1973 but weakened seriously in the early-mid 1980s and, as just about the country's only assured income, meant that since the state had become a country living entirely on unearned income from oil and gas, social programmes – such as healthcare and education – could not be assured.[42]

When Boumediène died in late 1978, life had improved for many and the country 'was one vast construction site.'[43] He 'had been mounting, with remarkable tenacity and skill, a protracted revolution within the revolution... the conversion of the Algerian people from a social and cultural patchwork into a nation, the transformation of a society so as to make it correspond to a state. With his death at the end of 1978 this process was aborted on the eve of its climax'; the *Révolution socialiste* came to an abrupt end and the development of the radical Islamist movement in Algeria dates from this time.

PRESIDENT CHADLI 1978-1988; ISLAMISTS FORM A POLITICAL PARTY

Boumediène's successor as President was Chadli Bendjedid: he had been trained as an officer in the French army, joining the Algerian army in 1955. The way in which he was chosen as President demonstrated how the *FLN* had become a facade behind which lay the power of the military hierarchy; an *FLN*

---

42   Algeria had been self-sufficient prior to independence, but by 2011, it imported 97% of its everyday needs: food, medicines, and so on (Lagarde, 2011, p 27).

43   Martinez, 2000, p 2, quoting Marc Cote, *L'Algérie* 1996 p 120.

Congress only had to ratify the choice.[44] Chadli was more discreet and less revolutionary than Boumediène and more of an administrator, but he was not the real power in the land. He just had to sign the contracts and other documents presented to him by Larbi Belkheir who, together with other military 'deciders', kept in the background; the government was told what it had to do.[45] Chadli had ceded real power to the *Sécurité militaire* (Military Security) and had broken the remaining power of the *FLN*.[46] The regime made its appeal to the middle class by moving to a capitalist programme, played to the West with great effect.

Early in his presidency, in a country with no traditions of organisation or management, two of Chadli's ministers decided that all businesses, large or small, had to be divided into two, three or even four, and Sonatrach – where all the existing managers were dismissed and went to foreign companies – was divided into about fifteen companies. The result was catastrophic,[47] as was what happened to Boumediène's policy of austerity, investment in industry and new jobs. Chadli stopped investment and allowed imports of all sorts, which delighted Algerians who could now buy what they wanted. But the world price of oil had fallen precipitously and the debts that Boumediène had incurred in building up industry had to be paid. The situation was disastrous for employment and has continued since that time: jobs were lost and there were no new ones to replace them.

Two events elsewhere in the world in 1979 were going to have a crucial influence in Algeria: the Iranian Revolution, which brought Ayatollah Khomeini to power, and the invasion of Afghanistan by

---

44   Stora, 2001, p 100.
45   Stora 2001, p 79; Malti 2010 p 268f writes that Belkheir accumulated a vast fortune estimated at more than a billion dollars which came from commissions for a variety of affairs, including the construction of the underwater gas pipeline from Algeria to Italy, the part of the fortune that he cornered from the elimination of Messaoud Zéghar in 1982 and from the import of wheat to Algeria, which he monopolised. Belkheir perpetuated his hold and those of his *DAF* (deserters from the French army) – companions who became the 'kernel' of those generals who organised the putsch against Chadli in January 1992.
46   Malti, 2010, p 281.
47   Malti, 2010, pp 253ff.

the Soviet Union. Saudi Arabia, aided and abetted by the USA, called for *mujahideen* to go and fight a religious war (*jihad*) to drive out the infidel Soviets. The *jihad* led to hundreds of young Algerians being recruited to go to Afghanistan in the 1980s; it was not apparent what a momentous effect this would have on Algeria and other states during the 1990s, following the defeat of the Soviets in Afghanistan and their downfall in 1989. It was the attacks of 9/11, in the USA in 2001, which really brought violent fundamentalist Islamism to the attention of much of the world. What happened in the response to that, when George W Bush decided on military action in the so-called 'War on Terrorism', was precisely what Osama Bin Laden and others had wanted in order to recruit followers to fight the infidel.[48] Thousands of mosques were built in Algeria, and a **family code**, adopted into law in May 1984,[49] was vigorously opposed, especially by women. It maintains polygamy, which was hardly an issue in society anymore, the prohibition of a woman to marry a non-Muslim and the requirement for a woman, even when an adult, to have a marriage 'guardian'. This was a massive concession to radical Islamist pressure.[50]

Chadli had to face up, in March 1980, to what became known as the *printemps berbère* (the Berber Spring), in Kabylia. This was caused by the government banning of the Kabyle Berber language at a conference in the University of Tizi Ouzou, the main town of Kabylia. It was the first time that a view different from that of Algerian unanimity had been put forward, and the appearance of a plural culture shook the *FLN* ideology of unity. There were serious riots, a severe crackdown and thirty deaths.[51]

---

48 Gilles Kepel, 2003, had researched what he called the 'political trail of Islamism' throughout the Muslim world up until the end of the 20th century. He found that it needed an extreme event to rejuvenate it. His book was published immediately before 9/11: his conclusion was extraordinarily prescient.

49 Akram Belkaïd, 2005, p 47, stated that the government, alarmed by the activity of militant Islamists, had given an order to *FLN* deputies to bring forward the vote for the adoption of the family code: the move was an attempt to cut the grass from under the feet of the Islamists, but it served instead to demonstrate government powerlessness. Women, in an official manner, became minors, he says.

50 Roberts, 2003 p 85.

51 Evans & Phillips, p 122.

I RETURN TO ALGIERS

In the mid-1980s, Algeria, financed by the World Bank – who planned to invite the international oil industry to explore for oil and gas there – requested bids for a major review of the prospects of finding more petroleum in the Algerian Sahara. This involved geological and allied work, and the contract was awarded to Robertson Research, the company for which I then worked in North Wales; it took myself – heading the project – and an Arabic-speaking colleague out to Algiers on several occasions over three or so years and gave rise to renewing my acquaintance with the country and people. It struck me how the city centre seemed to have changed not a jot in twenty-five years: the same buildings, some perhaps a little down-at-heel. But apart from changes in the names of streets,[52] and a monstrous new concrete hotel up on the slopes,[53] I seemed to recognise every stone. Little did I realise just how much was going to change very soon and how much I would become personally involved, if not in Algeria itself, starting with the momentous events of October 1988 and followed by the pivotal events of January 1992.

Looking back, there were signs when we were in Algiers that things were changing. One of these was perhaps that at the time we were making a presentation to Sonatrach staff – my colleague in Arabic[54] and myself in French – we were both asked instead to speak in English – a language that very few in the audience would have understood at that time. The language of business then was still very little but French. Was the request perhaps a political one?

---

52 These had been changed in 1962/3, but many of the old names continued to be used.
53 We stayed one night – the air conditioning didn't work, the atmosphere was foul, the service non-existent – and we decamped to the small old *Hotel Suisse* in the city.
54 My colleague spoke what is called standard Arabic, which would probably have been spoken by those who had been to university, not the local Algerian Arabic, which is very different.

3

VIOLENT RIOTS, AN ISLAMIST PARTY AND A THIRD COUP (1988-1992)

In early October 1988, there were serious riots in Algiers for the first time since independence; tanks appeared on the streets of Algiers and the army fired on crowds. The rioting had also spread to other towns. This event became a seminal point in the history of Algeria, leading to the recognition of an Islamist party – the *FIS* (*Front islamique du salut*) and to the terrible violence of the 1990s. President Chadli had moved to a capitalist programme, away from socialism towards democracy, and elections led to the possibility of the *FIS*, an Islamist political party, winning legislative elections. Because of this, the military cancelled the second round of elections in January 1992, leading to increasing violence and to massacres of civilians in the 1990s which shocked the world.

THE MILITARY FIRES ON CROWDS IN ALGIERS: HUNDREDS KILLED[1] (OCTOBER 1988)

Officially 150 were killed on the streets of Algiers in October 1988, but medical reports indicated 800, including many school

---

1   Based largely on accounts in Aggoun & Rivoire, p 116ff.

pupils and young people. How, and why, did this happen? Much remains clouded in mystery and there are varying interpretations.[2] What seems clear is that strikes in the second half of September 1988, which were over by the end of the month, had led to the rumour – nobody at the time knew who had spread it or why – of a general strike on Wednesday 5 October. At about ten that morning, Algiers exploded in violence. Big stores, cars and public buildings – which curiously were deserted by police for the whole day – were attacked by young people. They vandalised everything they met. The situation did not take long to get worse: nobody was controlling anything. The army began to encircle the city of Algiers in the early afternoon and protect important buildings, but otherwise apparently with instructions not to intervene. Meanwhile, the city was abandoned to a destructive fury.

A communiqué from the presidency announced a state of siege and that all civil, administrative and military authorities had been placed under military command. Friday morning appeared to show that calm had returned; the population started cleaning up the streets, and the midday Friday prayers were followed by a peaceful march. But this did not last. During the following days, the repression was terrible and spread to other towns – the call to the army had been fatal and, without qualms, soldiers obeyed orders, firing on civilians with all sorts of weapons, including heavy 23 mm machine guns mounted on tanks. Young people tried to defy the tanks with nothing in their hands. Confusion was added by persons firing automatic rifles before disappearing: who were they? Another question that has had no reply.

There were far too many questions. Why was there no attempt made on the first day to stop the general vandalism which got completely out of hand? Why had the army opened fire after calm had apparently returned on the Friday morning? But some questions have been answered. A major question had been: who had spread the rumour about the general strike and who had ordered pupils to come out and demonstrate? An article twenty years later – by

---

2   Stora in *Libération, 10 Oct 2008,* and others have written that the violence was largely spontaneous and/or that Islamists were behind it.

one of only a couple of Algerian human rights organisations at the time – states that the events were the result of a struggle for power between exasperated clans at the centre of power: the *FLN* and the Presidency. The *FLN*, he wrote, of which the *UGTA*[3] *(Union générale des travailleurs algériens* – Algerian workers' general union) was one of the mass organisations, incited 18,000 industrial workers to strike, knowing that it was the army that was really at the centre of power. General Khaled Nezzar, Minister of Defence, is said to have given the order to open fire in the streets of Algiers.[4]

Thousands of protesters, young people and those without political affiliation, who were mostly unemployed, were arrested and tortured; the mass revulsion against this torture, spearheaded by Algerian human rights organisations, led President Chadli to publicly condemn the torture and promise a new constitution which would inaugurate a multiparty state.[5] For the generals *('le pouvoir'*[6]*)* Ali Yahia says, repression can only be efficacious if it is pitiless and done in the greatest secrecy, outside of the fundamental essentials of the law and of basic human rights. Television, radio and press did not report information but only propaganda, with the objective of manipulating public opinion. The end justified the means for the perpetrators of repression, he says.

On Monday, 10 October, a big crowd gathered at Belcourt Mosque but, to avert more bloodshed, the religious leaders ordered them to go home; a reporter from *Le Monde* said that the crowds applauded the military, who moved away, but he proceeded to describe how later others came face to face with tanks, parachutists and other military and how a massacre came about. Various reporters immediately asked if the repression had not been 'coldly premeditated'. A further two questions: where were the water cannons which had been used against strikers at

---

3   Algerian workers' general union.
4   Aggoun & Rivoire, p 454.
5   AI report, 20426 Focus: Political Killings: Extrajudicial executions/Excessive use of lethal force/Deliberate and arbitrary killings by armed opposition groups. November 1993.
6   *Le Pouvoir* is a term given to those who take the major decisions in the country, for the most part, a small group of generals known as *'les décideurs'*.

the end of September, and why did tanks with 23 mm machine guns have to be used against youths and children in October? That same evening, President Chadli addressed the nation. The population was amazed to find that the very next day, shops were full of the promised cheap, subsidised food products which had been unobtainable, and that water was now flowing from taps – it had previously flowed for only two hours a day. On the downside, thousands of people had been arrested. Chadli deplored the loss of life, but nobody was ever held responsible for the repression and torture which took place.

During the 1980s, something quite remarkable had been happening in Algeria: the arrival of the *FIS* (*Front islamique du salut* – Islamic Salvation Front) as a political party was announced on 18 February 1989. Its principal leaders were Abassi Madani and Ali Benhadj, and the government legalised the movement seven months later.[7] For the first time, an Arab and Islamist country had authorised an Islamist party with the ambition of forming an Islamic State. The state had therefore chosen, during the presidency of President Chadli, to negotiate a *modus vivendi* with the Islamists, and by 1988/99, the *FIS* had embraced the democratic process; what happened in Algeria at this time is said to have caught the attention of the entire Muslim-majority world.[8] But by 1990, Saudi Arabian Wahabism had become a particularly virulent form of Islamism and as from the military *coup d'état* in January 1992, the state chose to portray, with a vengeance, all Islamists as unreasonable, intolerant, and the enemy of the Algerian people.[9]

Increasingly, 'radical Islamists... could exploit and benefit from the suspension of the democratic process, and the marginalisation of legitimate Islamist parties from the

---

7   Stora, *Les origines du Front islamique du salut* in *Reporters sans frontières*, 1996, p 175. The Algerian constitution in its National Charter of 27 Jun 1976 defined the position of Islam within its institutions stating that 'Islam is the religion of the State,' and that the president must be a Muslim. The Islamists, he writes, are in favour of the market economy and want to learn from the West how a society functions.

8   Le Sueur, 2010, p 38.

9   Roberts, 2003, p 112.

democratic process.'[10] This has been the tragedy of Algeria, where the vast majority were reasonable, tolerant people. Roberts' analyses show how wide of the mark is the widely held view that Islamism had the prime responsibility for the situation in the 1990s. He further shows that while the *FIS*, the political party that would have won the 1991-2 elections, as will be described, converted to democratic principles, the regime capitulated to external pressure – and particularly that coming from France.[11] Roberts saw not the slightest chance of a fully fledged Islamic state in Algeria, but it was just this view that led France to back the 'eradicators' rather than the 'conciliators' among the military, and to see the solution as one of injecting massive economic assistance. The real solution would have been a politically negotiated one, not a military and economic one.[12]

The future *FIS* had made its appearance on the Thursday when the respected Sheik Sahnoun put the blame for the crisis on a corrupt regime and said that it could only be resolved by

10   Le Sueur, 2010, p 122.
11   Roberts, 2003, p 160ff.
12   In July 1994, I wrote the following to the *Independent* in response to an editorial on 12 July:

Letter: Democracy is the cure for Algeria. 12 July 1994

Sir: You conclude (*Algerian crisis that threatens us all*; leading article, 12 July) that the best solution for Algeria to get out of its present crisis would be to reconstruct the economy. But can an economy be repaired where political stability has broken down? Thousands of people have been killed since January 1992 by the security forces, by Islamic groups and by other armed groups and individuals. The Algerian problem lies in poverty and social justice. The ruling party, recognising that something had to be done, called for a democratic general election, the first round of which was effectively won by the Islamic Salvation Front (*FIS*) in December 1991. It is questionable whether the *FIS* was extremist or anti-democratic at the time. A military coup followed and the second round of elections, scheduled for 16 January 1992, was cancelled. It is difficult to argue that the present appalling situation is better than to have allowed the democratic process to run its course.

President Zeroual has called for dialogue, but there is evidence that extremists on both sides have hijacked the country and in places uncontrolled terrorism reigns. This is ironic in a country that for years gave a lead in human rights issues.

The moderate voice of Islam has to be heard in Algeria and elsewhere. As you say, the Algerian crisis threatens us all. Governments cannot object to the democratic process when it produces results they do not like. Economies can better be repaired through the auspices of democratically elected governments than through dictatorships or autocracies ruling without the consent of their people.

Yours faithfully, R. W. GOLDSMITH

returning to Islam and the *Shari'a*. This was followed by Sheik Ali Belhadj, the imam of a mosque in Bab El-Oued, a popular quarter of Algiers, who would become the number two in the *FIS* and was regarded as the firebrand within the movement. He is reported to have said, "There is no democracy because the only power is Allah through the Koran, and not the people. If the people vote against the law of God, this is nothing other than blasphemy and in this case it is necessary to kill the non-believers for the good reason that they wish to substitute their authority for that of God."[13]

The *FIS* leaders later met with President Chadli and negotiated a return to calm: the riots and killings had allowed Islamists to acquire a legitimacy that no others had, and to show that only they could be intermediaries between the street and those in positions of power, *le pouvoir*. A new politically mature generation had arrived, while the events showed – by its use of such overwhelming and unnecessary firepower – that *le pouvoir* was ready to do all, including firing at children, to safeguard its privileges. At the same time, the charisma of Islamist activists, especially of Ali Belhadj, had been displayed and they had shown that they could play an important part in political matters. Stora[14] stated that the October demonstrations 'were largely spontaneous,' but Aggoun and Rivoire,[15] writing ten years later, argue that the military, supported, they say, by French President François Mitterand, had manipulated events.

The events that had erupted in October 1988 were followed by extraordinary changes: political parties were encouraged to form and be recognised, and an Islamist party took the lead: the press was virtually unfettered in what it could write. On the political side, the *FLN* and the *parti unique* had collapsed.[16] But Roberts[17] writes that within the Algerian elite, a consensus was in the process

---

13 The No 1 of the *FIS*, Dr Abassi Madani, was an older and politically moderate man. Roberts (2003, p 66f) wrote 'that it appears that (the two) leaders have been deliberately playing on several registers in order to accommodate several audiences and are consciously sustaining an intelligent double-act.'

14 Stora 1994 p 81.

15 Aggoun & Rivoire, 2004, pp 116-134.

16 Stora, 1994, p 80.

17 Roberts, 2003, p 34ff.

of being organised which would obtain a new lease of life for the state and for the *FLN* as the necessary guarantor of the state. 'The state which the *FLN* created, the armed forces, the civil service, the diplomatic corps and the intelligence and security organs (were) still very much in place.' However, it was the armed forces which had complete hegemony.

Chadli was the only candidate for presidential elections in December 1988. A new constitution bringing an end to the monopoly of the *FLN* followed in February 1989 and, as a result of the introduction of pluralism, forty-four political parties were formed in the next two years. Algeria entered a period of openness, democratic freedom and freedom of the press which would last for three years. However, the *FLN*, which – led by the President – had acted as an oppressive restraint on the public, had also acted as a restraint on the army. But now army commanders were no longer members of the *FLN*: there was no longer a restraint on the military and they could no longer be held to account.[18] The military then forced President Chadli, who had also been the Minister of Defence, to surrender this top job to the then Chief of Staff, Khaled Nezzar. The effect of this appointment will become only too apparent: Nezzar was the most powerful man in Algeria. Roberts[19] summarised the change which took place in 1989 as 'the replacement of one, relatively orderly (because primarily political), variety of authoritarian rule by another, militaristic, manipulative, immeasurably more violent, unquestionably less legitimate and correspondingly less effective, variety.' There had been no movement whatsoever towards democracy.[20]

The new 1989 constitution was approved in a referendum: this had many reforms, including Article 45 which guaranteed detained persons immediate access to their families. Several international

---

18   Roberts, 2003, p 253.
19   Roberts, 2003 p 254.
20   This is a quite different view from that of William Quandt, who concluded (*Between Ballots and Bullets; Algeria's Transition from Authoritarianism*, 1998) that the 1989 constitution signaled the end of the old authoritarian system, or at any rate the beginning of a transition to a non-authoritarian form of government. The following ten years from 1998 clearly vindicate Roberts' interpretation.

major human rights treaties were also ratified, including the International Covenant on Civil and Political Rights (ICCPR), and the Convention against Torture and Other Cruel, Inhuman or Degrading Treatment or Punishment. These treaties were, as will be seen, ignored in future years. This did not prevent the Algerian authorities boasting, in the 1990s, that they had a better human rights record than Britain, since Algeria had signed more treaties.

ISLAMISTS WIN DEMOCRATIC ELECTIONS BUT OUSTED IN MILITARY PUTSCH

The *FIS* went on to win municipal and regional elections in June 1990, with 54% of the votes against the *FLN*'s 18%, and gained much support for its social work: it was the *FIS* that brought assistance after a major earthquake, while the government was nowhere to be seen. AI[21] noted that torture almost ceased during this time; it really was a period when Algerians had hope for a better future.

Despite a law which did not allow the formation of political parties based solely on religion, four Islamic parties were recognised: the *Front islamique du salut (FIS), al-Nahda,*[22] *Hamas*[23] and *al-Umma*. The *FIS* gained much support for its call for justice and for its attack on maladministration and government corruption. The Prime Minister, Mouloud Hamrouche, in the months prior to the local elections in June 1990, not only tolerated the *FIS*'s activities, including violent activities that breached the law, but bolstered the *FIS*'s electoral appeal while sabotaging that of his own party, the *FLN*.[24]

---

21   Report 20426, November 1993.
22   *Al-Nahda (MNI) Mouvement de la Nahda Islamique:* Movement for Islamic Renaissance.
23   Nothing to do with the Palestinian group of the same name.
24   Roberts, 2003, p 84f; Roberts says that what Hamrouche did was by no means unique – he cites Prime Minister Abdelhamid Brahimi, who brought in the controversial pro-Islamist 'Family Code' in 1984 and then in 1990, just before the local elections, announced that *FLN* corruption in government had cost the country $26 billion over the years, the equivalent of the total debt.

But in these same years, 1989 to 1991, the state of the economy worsened,[25] international debt increased and worldwide oil prices dropped following the first Gulf war (August 1990 to February 1991); Algeria's revenues came, and continue to come, almost entirely from oil and gas, and the country suffered from this loss of income. The International Monetary Fund and World Bank were called in; this led to a massive reduction of the number of employees in public enterprises, 50% devaluation of the Algerian dinar and privatisations. Prices increased by 50-200%. All this led to great difficulties for the ordinary Algerian, and frustrations among the young and the impoverished got worse.[26] Despite this, there was no Islamist onslaught on the state: the Islamist movement sought to advance its cause *within* the framework of the Algerian state and it was not, as was put forward by nearly all international opinion, a revolutionary movement – although it did use fiery rhetoric and to this extent was hypocritical. The first Gulf war, following Saddam Hussein's invasion of Kuwait, did, however, radicalise Algerian public opinion against the West and complicated Algerian politics by diverting Algerians from their own political preoccupations; the crisis of the war was a major challenge to Algeria's attempt to move towards democracy.[27]

---

25 Stora, 1994, p 84ff. Hocine Malti (2010 p 263f) wrote that whereas Boumediène had followed a policy of austerity and of investment in industry and new jobs (there was almost nothing to buy in shops), Chadli stopped investment and allowed imports of all sorts. Algerians were delighted to be able to buy what they wanted, but the world price of oil had fallen precipitously: the debts that Boumediène had incurred in building up industry had to be paid. The situation was catastrophic: jobs were lost and there have been no new ones to replace them.

26 Given this situation, Roberts points out that it is abnormal to the point of being bizarre that the FIS, while committed above all to helping the poor, seemed to have no views about the economy of the country. A senior FIS representative whom I met in Paris in July 1997, through the Amnesty France Country Coordinator for Algeria, said that a very significant gap within the FIS leadership was that nobody had any experience of economics.

27 Evans and Phillips (p 162f) describe how far the FIS's support for Iraq's Saddam Hussein had radicalised Algerian politics; Chadli and his Prime Minister, Hamrouche, believed that the Gulf War had fatally wounded the FIS and would bring an FLN victory: misjudging the situation, they changed the electoral system and gave rise to the possibility of an overwhelming victory for the FIS.

PRESIDENT CHADLI FORCED OUT IN A 'COUP D'ETAT'

National elections should have taken place in June 1991 but were postponed, and the two *FIS* leaders, Abassi Madani and Ali Belhadj, were imprisoned on trumped-up charges.[28] Abdelkader Hachani led the *FIS* in the legislative elections of 1991/92 which were arranged as in France: the first round took place on 26 December 1991, and the *FIS* were apparently left in a situation where they would win a massive victory. There are two important conclusions to be noted, however: firstly, the elections had taken place in a reasonably democratic fashion – the most democratic of all those held since independence. Secondly, there were massive abstentions – the *FIS* received a million votes less than in the local elections of June 1990. They had, as a result, despite gaining 181 seats out of 231 seats during the first round, obtained less than 25% of the eligible votes. The number of abstentions has led, together with the suspicion that many *FIS* votes could well have been protest votes against the *FLN*, to the conclusion that the *FIS* did not win so much support as has been supposed. Critically, they alienated the francophone middle class, many of whom fled the country, while at the same time the *FLN* was in disarray.[29] The victory was due, according to Martinez,[30] to an opportunistic coalition of four groups: military entrepreneurs (*ALN* officers who turned to business), petty traders, such as butchers and grocers, *hittistes* (those who are unemployed and 'who prop up the wall') and fourthly, devout Muslim activists. There were a variety of political, economic and social choices and issues at stake, all providing motives to vote for the *FIS*.

The *FIS* was set to become the government, but the military cancelled the second round of elections due in mid-January 1992 and forced President Chadli, who was ready to 'cohabit'[31]

---

28   Roberts, 2003, p 79 & 178, questions the motives of army commanders in confronting the *FIS* in mid-June 1991.

29   Evans and Phillips, p 158ff.

30   Martinez 2000, p 23.

31   A French expression used when the president and government are from different political parties.

with the *FIS*, to resign. Malti (2010 p 293) writes that it was the true 'deciders', Belkheir, Khaled Nezzar, Mohamed Lamari and 'Tewfik',[32] who obliged Chadli to resign. The military did this, they said, to 'safeguard democracy' but had no intention of publically assuming responsibility for governing the country. Prime Minister Hamrouche also lost his job, which had no doubt been one of the aims of the military. The primacy of the armed forces over the executive and Presidency was revealed; little changed when – seven years later, a civilian, Abdelaziz Bouteflika, was chosen (by the military) to be President in 1999 after extraordinary delays and no doubt behind-the-scenes machinations.

There is no doubt that in cancelling the second round of elections, the military had the blessing of France, the United States and other western governments. The events of late 1979 in Iran, which had brought the Ayotollah Khomeini to power, had been traumatic for the West, and they made the error of thinking that the same thing could happen again in Algeria in 1992.[33] There is no question that events in the Middle East during the 1980s – Saddam Hussein's attack on Iran in 1980 and the appalling eight-year war that followed, and the US attack on Iraq following Saddam Hussein's invasion of Kuwait in 1990, had repercussions in Algeria – but there had been no threat of an Islamic Republic of the Iranian type.

The immediate actions of the authorities following their cancellation of the elections were to ban the *FIS*, to impose a state of emergency – which remained in force for nearly twenty years – and to arrest some 10,000 Islamist sympathisers and militants who were imprisoned in the Sahara for years under atrocious conditions.[34]

---

32 Or 'Toufik'.
33 Roberts, 2003, p 111, points out that this was a misreading of the situation, Algeria being in no way comparable to Iran.
34 They had committed no crime but were regarded by the authorities as 'dangerous' (shades of the later notorious Guantanamo). President Zeroual, who came to office at the end of November 1995, made his first gesture of conciliation when he closed the last camps (ANH 8 Jan 1996). Algeria-Watch (26 Jul 2010: *Les déportés des camps du Sud, une plaie qui continue de saigner*) states that human rights associations estimate the number interned for some weeks up to four years as between 10,000 and 24,000. Hundreds of ex-internees suffered from exposure to high levels of radiation due to French nuclear tests 1960-1967. The internees returned to their homes, often to be stigmatised as terrorists.

ASSASSINATION OF NEW PRESIDENT; ALGIERS AIRPORT BOMBED

The cancellation of the elections on 11 January 1992 has been described as a *coup d'état* and Chadli resigned. He was replaced by an *Haut Comité d'État* (High Committee of State) which called on **Mohamed Boudiaf,** *chef historique* of the *FLN* and exiled in Morocco for twenty-eight years, to become Head of State. They must have expected a malleable person but found instead that they had brought into Algeria a man who wanted both 'a united and just society' and to reform the system. He didn't last long and was assassinated six months later, on 29 June, in front of live television cameras. He was speaking of his objective of making Algeria an open democratic country. The assassin was one of those responsible for guarding him; he and others were duly found guilty in 1995, but few believed this.

A commission of enquiry admitted that the assassin had not acted alone and pointed to 'clans in power' – this was quite normal, provided no names were named.[35] Those who could have expected to lose their jobs under Boudiaf – Belkheir, Nezzar and Médiène – and the rest of the high military command, knew that nobody would now question their position. Moreover, they were fully supported by France, who – together with other western countries – had no wish to see the *FIS* in government. Akram Belkaïd[36] wrote that everybody now knew the punishment that awaited them if they made a frontal attack on the interests of *le pouvoir*. Mohamed Boudiaf had been brought in 'to save Algeria'. For the Algerian street, *'ils l'ont amené et ils l'ont tué'* ('they brought him here and they killed him')'; 29 June 1992 was the day that a curse came upon Algeria. After this date it was total, inhumane war.[37]

The assassination of Mohamed Boudiaf brought to the fore the division within the Algerian power structure. There were those, known as *les* éradicateurs, who were convinced that

---

35 Aggoun and Rivoire, pp 291-2.
36 Belkaïd, 2005, p 21.
37 El-Kadi Ihsane, *Le Quotidien d'Oran*, 27 Jun 2002, writing ten years after the assassination.

the only way to go was by means of a brutal suppression of the Islamist movement, and those, *les conciliateurs,* who believed that compromise must be negotiated if the state was to be preserved. The 'eradicators' were supported by Paris and the bulk of the Algerian French-language press, but had little support among the mass of the Algerian population.[38] Not only was there a division among the generals, but also among Islamists, between the *FIS* and a group committed to violence to bring down the state, the *Groupe(s) islamique armé(s)* (*GIA* **Armed Islamic Group**).

Two months after the assassination, **a bomb o**n 26 August 1992 at **Algiers Airport**, which killed nine people and injured 128, may help illustrate the difficulty of understanding what was going on.[39] The attack was condemned by most political parties, including the *FIS,* who denounced it and said that 'combattants of Islam were not authorised to attack without having most carefully defined their objectives with respect to Islamic rules.' It was troubling that the security forces had received warning of the attack and had evacuated their own members, but had not warned the general public in the hall where the attack took place. Despite its condemnation, the *FIS* was discredited both nationally and internationally, and allowed General Belkheir to put new anti-terrorism[40] legislation in place and make it impossible for dialogue with the *FIS* to be renewed. But who then was responsible? Suspicion fell on other Islamist groups, but Roger Foligot, a specialist on French security matters, reported in the *Journal du dimanche*[41] that the French security forces had been rapidly convinced that the Algerian *DRS* *(Direction des renseignments et de la sécurité* – Department for Information and Security)[42] was responsible for the attack. The

---

38   Roberts, 2003, p 155f.

39   Aggoun and Rivoire, p 295ff.

40   Terrorism or terrorists are much-used words that are almost impossible to define. I have tried, throughout this book, not to use them except in a quote.

41   28 Aug 1993.

42   Until 1990, when its name was officially changed, the *DRS* had been known as the *Sécurité militaire* (*SM*). Twenty years later, and more, the *DRS* is still called the *SM* by many.

Algerian authorities said, some days later, that they had arrested four Islamists implicated in the attack. These admitted that they were the attackers but then, despite more threats, also revealed the torture they had undergone in order to make them admit responsibility; all were condemned and executed.[43] It transpired that one of the men, Djamel Laskri, who it was claimed had taken part in the attack, had been in prison at the time.

This brief analysis demonstrates the web of claims and counter-claims and the difficulty of establishing the truth: it begins to illustrate the complexity of the situation.

As an unsatisfactory generalisation, Algeria divided into two camps: those sympathetic to the *FIS* and/or Islamists, and those – an increasing number as the decade wore on – who were not. For the state-controlled television (which was all that there was until the arrival of illegal satellite dishes and *Al Jazeera*[44]), for Algerian radio and for much of the 'independent' media, Islamists were always responsible. For the other side, *le pouvoir* was responsible. For many – perhaps most – matters were simple, and internationally this was to a large extent true too: most reporters would not have the time to dig into matters and try and understand what was going on; besides, they were not permitted to do so: foreign journalists were obliged to be accompanied by police, ostensibly for their safety but in practice to ensure that they did not go to the 'wrong' places, ask awkward questions and interview those who might provide the 'wrong' information.[45]

The Algerian military had learned lessons well from the Soviet KGB, and one could have the impression that the only efficient institution, in a country of chaos, was that of the security forces. News appearing in the Algerian media relating to violence and

---

43 Officially, Algeria has not executed any of those condemned to death since a moratorium was announced in 1993.

44 *Al Jazeera* was set up in Qatar in 1996, employing ex-BBC staff who had been employed in Saudi Arabia until the station there was closed down by the Saudis. *Al Jazeera* was a highly reputable broadcaster for many years, but since at least 2012, it has been controlled by the Qatari government and is no longer editorially independent.

45 I remember Robert Fisk, one of the most notable British investigative journalists at the time, making this point.

security matters, from which European and US reports were predominantly derived, was strictly controlled by the Algerian authorities, who made sure that their story was the one that was circulated worldwide. Propaganda was put out by all: how was it possible for the ordinary citizen to have any reasonable idea of what was truly going on? It was not, and he or she could not. The targets of attacks by Islamist armed groups in the early years – at least it was assumed to be by them – were the military and security forces, then intellectuals, journalists,[46] professionals and a few foreigners.

In a paper written as early as 1992, Roberts recognised that the West's reactions to what had been happening in Algeria over the previous four years were based on the most superficial analysis, and showed not the slightest understanding of the situation in the country.[47] Western commentary exaggerated the importance of economic motivations ('bread riots' due to price rises, for example) and the idea of 'Islamic fundamentalism'. No notice was taken of 'the question of public exasperation with arbitrary government, and the concomitant demand for a form of government based on the rule of law.' False analogies were made with the Soviet Union and Iran. The West painted the *FLN* as in a state of decadence, which Roberts states was not so, and suggested that the *FIS* would transform Algeria into a fully fledged Islamic Republic, just like Iran. There was no reasonable comparison to be made between what had happened in Iran in 1979 and the situation in Algeria in January 1992.

HUMAN RIGHTS ATROCITIES: AMNESTY INTERNATIONAL (AI) RAISES ITS CONCERNS

The 'coup' in January 1992 and the violence and human rights atrocities that followed had led to AI much increasing its work

---

46   AI, in its report AI MDE 28/36/97 stated that, 'In May 1995, after meeting AI delegates, Mohamed Abderrahmani, editor of the pro-government daily *El Moudjahid,* said: "I hope I will see you again, you never know if I will be alive tomorrow." The next morning, he was assassinated in his car as he drove his children to school.'

47   Republished in Roberts, 2003, p 106ff.

on Algeria and to visiting in March and December 1992 to discuss its concerns with government officials.[48]

As I have already noted, because of my previous experience of Algeria in the 1960s and 1980s, and since I also had experience of previous Amnesty work on Syria and Bolivia, I was asked in late 1993 to take on the voluntary job of what was called 'Amnesty International UK Country Coordinator, Algeria'. The work of a country coordinator was to work for professional staff in the International Secretariat and AIUK on a country where human rights atrocities were of concern, to learn about these and to encourage other AI groups in the UK to write to senior politicians and others whom we knew wanted to try and do something about these. Later, they wrote to families and politicians in Algeria.

In the 1990s, AIUK Country Coordinators were members of a team led by the professional staff at the International Secretariat, the worldwide hub then of all Amnesty research work. That of Algeria was headed by the Researcher for Algeria, Donatella Rovera, and subsequently by Philip Luther.[49] The staff had daily telephone contact with Algerians in the country and met many of them when they visited Algeria in the early years, and they had a number of staff working with and assisting them. Donatella had valuable personal contacts within Algeria who provided information about what was happening there. She went on what were called missions to the country to visit such people and government officials when AI had received Algerian government approval to do this – needless to say, the reports that were published did not appeal to the Algerian government, and visiting the country became more difficult as time went by.[50]

---

48   This could be done at that time and for some few years later, but then it became impossible to obtain visas. AI never visited, except with permission of the Algerians.

49   AI had valuable contacts within Algeria, and Donatella Rovera visited the country to visit such people when AI had received government approval to do this – needless to say, visiting the country became more difficult as time went by and AI produced reports damning – in the most careful prose – what was going on there.

50   There was a furore much later when the Algerian press reported that AI had asked to visit General Mohammed Lamari. Was it perhaps following this that the authorities would not issue visas to AI staff?

Donatella and her staff kept Country Coordinators around the world regularly informed, at least weekly, of what was going on and in days prior to access to the web sent out paper copies of relevant articles from newspapers, weekly magazines and others, which reported significant human rights abuses. I then summarised the material into a four-page bi-monthly newsletter[51] which I forwarded to the fourteen or so UK local groups[52] and to coordinators in Western Europe, the USA, Canada, Africa and elsewhere. This provided background information from the press from Europe and Algeria and encouraged groups to send letters to Algerian government officials and others. Many of these letters called on the President and ministers to take action to prevent such atrocities. In general, there was no reply, but a group in New Zealand received a personal letter from President Bouteflika inviting them to visit Algeria.[53] At intervals, groups were asked to write to Algerian authorities appealing for the release of individuals; each group usually communicated with the family of a specific 'disappeared'[54] relative and a few could build up a special relationship with them. I shall write in some detail about the 'disappeared' and explain how we tried to assist in obtaining truth and justice for them, or at least did our best to publicise throughout Britain, and other countries around the world, what was happening in Algeria beyond that which was published in the British press or through television.

I also worked together with staff in the British part of the organisation (AIUK).[55] This included writing, or proposing, letters for the national press, regular visits, almost weekly, to the Foreign Office, primarily to the Algeria Desk Officer, and included briefing outgoing ambassadors to Algeria, visits to Parliament,

---

51   This was called *Algeria News Highlights* (ANH) and has been used in this compilation.

52   From Truro to Glasgow, working on Algerian disappearances and other cases.

53   The letter arrived in New Zealand in 1999 in a remarkable envelope, decorated with gold braid or some such finery. This was early in Bouteflika's presidency and was not repeated.

54   In the 1990s, we wrote of the 'disappeared', but later the inverted commas were omitted. The more expressive term *enforced disappearance* is now used.

55   In a separate building a short walk away – until AIUK moved its office in the early 2000s.

Commons and Lords.[56] AIUK had a much smaller staff then, and it was not long before I was the AIUK representative to visit the Foreign Office, MPs and peers in the House of Lords and others.[57] Several British MEPs in Brussels or Strasbourg were most concerned about the situation in Algeria: one in particular, the Conservative MEP for South London, would, when he had heard some news about Algeria that particularly concerned him, telephone and ask for a motion to be prepared which he would then bring before the European Parliament. These were occasions when the Algerian authorities really reacted – it was evident that they took the criticisms seriously and expressed their unhappiness publicly. Back in Britain, a group of four of us from the Refugee Council, the Medical Foundation for the Care of Victims of Torture[58] (now 'Freedom from Torture'), and AI, led by the Director of the United Nations Association in Britain, would call on the Foreign Secretary and the Minister for Middle East and North Africa when they were about to visit Algiers to update them on the situation and urge them to take up our concerns when speaking to ministers there. I also worked closely with the French Country Coordinator in Paris and the Dutch in Amsterdam. In Paris, I attended meetings in AI France offices, was introduced to the leaders of Algerian political parties in France and met French journalists. I had close contact with other Algeria Country Coordinators in Western Europe and the USA.[59] We coordinators from around the world met together

---

56 Lord (Eric) Avebury was a particularly valuable contact: it seemed he spent all of his time campaigning on human rights, and most particularly Algeria, and I was frequently invited to lunch, to update him on Algeria, and to debates in the House of Lords.

57 A number of peers took a particular interest in Algeria – it was apparent that they (and MEPs) had more time to spend on AI matters than did members of the House of Commons.

58 Experienced doctors there told me that they had never, at that time, seen such terrible wounds as those of the victims coming from Algeria. Up to 1999 they had treated some seventy survivors.

59 For nearly all the eleven years that I worked for AI on Algeria, I compiled two-monthly summaries of news about Algeria selected from Algerian, French and British newspapers. These were circulated to AI groups worldwide and to other interested individuals, including the Foreign Office North African staff, members of both Houses of Parliament with whom I had very close contact and others.

in London (twice) and in the Netherlands. Through the Society for Algerian Studies in London and other international academic meetings around Britain, I also got to know some Algerians and some British experts, university researchers and graduates.

I carried out this work for Amnesty, which turned out to be a full-time job, from January 1994 to November 2004. Thereafter, I assisted Nassera Dutour, whose experience of having a disappeared son led her to quite extraordinary efforts on behalf of families of 'enforced disappearances' in Algeria. I helped her primarily by providing English translations of her detailed quarterly newsletters of the *Collectif des Familles de Disparus en Algérie (CFDA)*.[60]

---

60   The *CFDA* website address: http://www.algerie-disparus.org/

4

LA SALE GUERRE[1] (CIVIL WAR 1992-2004)

The cancellation of democratic elections, the forcing-out of Chadli, the appearance of armed Islamic groups, militia and bombings and the violent reaction from the military set the scene for the appalling 1990s decade of violence that followed. There were the most terrible atrocities: some 200,000 were killed, 15,000 to 20,000 people 'disappeared' and up to 1.5 million people were forcibly displaced.[2] Algeria divided into camps: those who were, or had been, sympathetic to the banned *FIS* and those – an increasing number as the decade wore on – who were not. The Algerian authorities made sure that it was their story that was the one that was circulated worldwide. They claimed that the Islamist *GIA*, many of whose fighters had been trained in Afghanistan and whose aim was the establishment of an Islamic state by force of arms, was

---

1   *The Dirty War* – The title of Habib Souaïdia's book that woke much of France to what was going on in Algeria in the 1990s.

2   François Gèze et Salima Mellah, *Algeria-Watch, Algérie. L'impossible justice transitionnelle*. 26 Feb 2019.

responsible. It was probably they who carried out most of the atrocities, but as early as 1994 there were indications of infiltration of the *GIA* by the military.

It is extraordinary that as early as 1993 the highly respected Editor of *Le Matin*, Saïd Mekbel, savagely opposed to political Islam, had said that he understood that the true person behind the killings of intellectuals in the early 1990s was the head of the secret political police Major-General Mohammed Médiène, called 'Tewfik'. He wrote that if he himself was killed it would be on the order of 'Tewfik'.[3] Despite the precautions that he took, Mekbel could not escape being assassinated on 3 December 1994. Ninety-four Algerian journalists were assassinated in the early 1990s.

It may be helpful at this stage to look at the protagonists of the 1990s: the main Islamist armed groups and the military, security forces and militias which opposed them, and then at how the civilian population was managing to live under these conditions. We shall then return to review the violence in France as well as Algeria, and how Amnesty became involved in bringing its human rights concerns in Algeria to international attention.

ARMED ISLAMIST GROUPS AND THE MILITARY SECURITY (SM/DRS)

Three million *FIS* voters felt disenfranchised following the military putsch in January 1992. For the next two years, young men especially sought to join armed groups or bring political change; they expected the regime would be rapidly overthrown. A myriad of small clandestine groups were formed,[4] but for much of the first decade, there were only two of real significance: the

---

3   Reported in an interview published fourteen years after his death (Hocine Malti, Algeria-Watch, 10 Jan 2015). http://www.algeria-watch.org/fr/aw/malti_fin_de_ regne.htm quoting from Monika Borgmann, Saïd *Mekbel* : une mort à la lettre, Tétraèdre, Paris, p. 101. And Algeria-Watch, Vingt ans après : décembre 1994, *l'assassinat de Saïd Mekbel, le journaliste qui avait dû "avaler ce qu'il sait"*.

4   Labat p 227.

GIA and the *AIS* (*Armée islamique du salut* – **Islamic Salvation Army**).[5]

The result of its bloodthirsty acts was that the *GIA* attracted all the media attention, while other more responsible groups were hardly recognised. This was particularly so of the *AIS*,[6] which was formed later – in 1994 – as the armed wing of the *FIS* with the objective of forcing the regime to relegalise the *FIS*.[7] Its aim was to destroy the Algerian military and security forces; it realised that a guerilla campaign would be insufficient and that the *GIA* would be unsuccessful relying uniquely on violence. They also realised that the *GIA* risked exasperating people with its deadly ideology, and announced that the *AIS* 'leads the movement within the strict bounds of the Islamic *Shari'a* which forbids the killing of the innocent, mutilation of victims and attacks on those who are not concerned in the conflict, whether they are men or women, children or adults, Muslims or non-Muslims, Algerians or foreigners.'[8] Media attention was placed largely on the much more violent *GIA*. The question has to be asked whether the *AIS* effort to rehabilitate the *jihad* had not come too late: popular support for the cause had undoubtedly weakened.

In 1997, the *AIS* admitted it could not obtain its aim – to return the *FIS* to legality and power – through violence; its national 'emir' ordered combat operations to cease on 1 October and called upon other groups to respond.[9] The call for a truce coincided with the release of *FIS* leaders, and it was hoped that this would be a turning point. But the *GIA* was in no mood to

5   There were two other groups: the *MIA* (*Mouvement islamique armée*), formed in 1992-3, which – like the *GIA* – had the aim of establishing an Islamic state by force of arms (Roberts, 2003, p 269) and the *MEI* (*Mouvement pour un État Islamique*), formed well before January 1992. There was evidently no unanimity among the four Islamist groups.

6   This paragraph is based primarily on Martinez, p 197ff; in 1995, the *AIS* may have had 40,000 men (p 202).

7   Roberts, 2003, p 269.

8   Quoted by Martinez, p 202 from a collection of *AIS-FIS* letters, entitled *Mots de vérité à ceux qui se sentent concernés*, edited by the *FIS* overseas executive, Apr 1995.

9   Martinez, pp 18-19.

follow suit, nor were other clans in the army. President Zeroual resigned[10] and this was followed by hundreds of villagers being massacred in events that shook the world at the time. The *AIS* was officially disbanded in early 2000.

The original aim of the *GIA* in early 1992 had been the establishment of an Islamic state by force of arms.[11] It classified all individuals as either 'enemies of Islam' or supporters of the *jihad,* and hence civilians were called upon to choose sides under pain of death.[12] The regime was illegitimate and had to be destroyed. This brought religion into what was at heart a political battle, and the *GIA* went to war against all who kept the regime in power; the security forces, government departments, the education system and foreigners all apparently became legitimate targets. The various armed groups of the *GIA* and 'emirs' had complete autonomy and as a result attracted fanatics impelled by hatred of the regime rather than more competent young men, who went elsewhere.

The *GIA* was claimed by the Algerian authorities as the prime Islamist armed group responsible for atrocities. But who and what was the *GIA*? And to what extent is it possible that at least some atrocities might have been hatched within the **Securité militaire (DRS)** – the feared political police of the military hierarchy? There has always been a great deal of speculation about the *GIA*: as early as January 1994, *Jeune Afrique*[13] stated that it seemed to be a convenient mask that camouflaged the real authors.[14] Already by this time there were indications of infiltration by the

10 Imad Boubekri wrote nineteen years later, on 12 Jan 2016, in Facebook TSA *Tout sur l'Algérie* (http://www.algeria-watch.org/fr/article/hist/1992/betchine_accuse.htm) that retired General Betchine explained that he had decided to break the silence about what happened in the 1990s and said "They torpedoed the negotiations that I was leading at the time for President Zeroual with Abassi Madani and Ali Belhadj... It was them who know how and why Zeroual left *le pouvoir*. It's them..." (never citing whom) "...who put the pressure on him and pushed us to quit *le pouvoir.*"
11 Roberts, 2003, p 269.
12 This paragraph is based on Martinez, p 207-8.
13 27 Jan-2 Feb 1994, on which some of these notes are based.
14 Roberts, 2003, page 154-5, states that it began to make its presence known in mid-1993 and 'and has been a massive embarrassment to the *FIS.*'

military. According to the Algerian authorities, the *GIA* was part of the *FIS*; according to the *FIS* the *GIA* was really an arm of the military junta.

The main source of information about the *GIA* was said to be a weekly called *Al-Ansar*, edited in Poland and broadcast from Peshawar in Pakistan. This was before *al-Qaida* had been heard of, and I used to comment for some years, when speaking on Algeria, about the 'Afghan influence' in the country and elsewhere.[15] The recruiting, arming and training of *mujahideen* by Saudi Arabia and the USA to defeat the USSR in Afghanistan in 1989 has had the most terrible repercussions around the world, as we now know.[16] Algeria has certainly suffered greatly: maybe it would have done so whatever happened, but the return of hundreds of unemployed Algerians who had been trained and indoctrinated in Afghanistan – where they had gone to become martyrs – only added to the potential for suffering. Labat[17] states that the *GIA* was founded on a system of allegiance – to the area, district or town, but small groups welcomed combatants from the Afghan *maquis*; these provided its leaders and an ideology for the *GIA*.

Recruitment for the *GIA* was straightforward: those who joined were in the majority sixteen to twenty-five years old, coming from a society where some 60% of that age were unemployed with no prospect of a job, many excluded from the education system; they would have no hope of their own housing nor much hope of marriage – their expectation of

15   This refers to the large number of young Algerians and Egyptians who had been attracted to fight in Afghanistan for the *mujahadeen* against the Soviets and other *infidels*. They returned to North Africa unemployed and were easy pickings for armed groups.

16   In 1996, both the USA and Pakistan supported the Taliban in Afghanistan, armed and funded by the Pakistani secret service, the ISI (Kepel p 11). Kepel writes that 'for Washington and Islamabad, it scarcely seemed to matter that a retrograde version of Islam in its most literal and ossified form daily trampled the rights of men and women into the dust.'

17   Séverine Labat: This note and most of the following two paragraphs are from *Le GIA* in *Reporters sans frontières*, p 182ff. *Le drame algérien* is a remarkable book: articles written by some thirty-six of the principal French and Algerian writers on the violence of the first years of the 1990s. It was published as early as August 1996.

political change had gone with the suppression of the *FIS*. In short, they were young people without hope for the future. Life as a member of the *GIA* would have offered them reason to live – however perverted in our eyes – and die; it would have provided an opportunity to *casser un flic* (to beat up a policeman), it could have provided excitement, companionship, a hard but, for them, rewarding life and, very likely, death.

If the *GIA* was directed by 'Afghans' who had come back from Afghanistan, what was its relationship to *le pouvoir*? The unfolding of this story will provide clues and very serious questions about what was going on. The *GIA's* stated aims of demonising the 'enemies of Islam' included Christians and Jews, and it followed that the French also became a target. Antagonism between Arabic speakers and French speakers deepened; the latter represented everything from which the young were excluded – the educational system, mastery of the language which was needed to succeed (French), access to a privileged situation in Europe… Convinced that they were the victims of the francophones who were responsible for the ills from which they suffered, this view was reinforced by the Algerian and western press, which emphasised the assassination of intellectuals and others while hardly recognising the violence of the regime. The *GIA mujahideen* was going to put right social ills and the interruption of the electoral process. By the publication of *fatwa,* they defined what was, in their eyes, permitted or not; they 'prohibited' the sale of cigarettes, the playing of music, television satellites, required women to wear the *hijab*… announced sentence of death on those who did not submit to their authority. Hundreds of schools were destroyed. More than 500 women were victims of violence, mutilations and rape in a little more than three years.[18] The struggle with the regime meant new loyalties, and the family, which had always been considered sacrosanct, could be cast aside because *jihad* was said to be above ties of blood; there was no longer respect for family, elders and their principles.

---

18   These figures continue to be from Labat's *Le GIA* in *Reporters sans frontières,* p 184.

Many **'emirs'** were far removed from the religious Islamic militants: some were very young men of fifteen to eighteen who worked with small groups carrying Kalashnikovs and became notorious. But they gained control of areas of Greater Algiers, faced certain death, and there was always someone to replace them. Despite envy and jealousy of them, they retained a certain respect and attractiveness. Their enemies were at first intellectuals, teachers and journalists. At the same time, they stopped crime and restored order.[19] It was therefore simplistic to view this as just a fight against an irreligious regime.[20] Successful 'emirs' were able to abandon the beard and take on lucrative 'import-export' businesses, allowing the prospect of *jihad* and trade liberalisation to provide them with honourable and profitable outcomes of the violence.[21]

The way in which recruitment took place within the *GIA* made it easy for the *Sécurité militaire* to infiltrate it. Mohamed Samraoui, who had been a colonel and the number two in Algerian counter-espionage, defected from the *DRS* in 1996. His book, *Chroniques des années de sang,*[22] published in 2003, caused a furore.[23] He wrote that Djamel Zitouni, *GIA* chief, was in the pay of the generals, and said that there were three GIAs: one consisting of extremists and others, one infiltrated by the *DRS* (*Sécurité militaire*), in which he served, and another formed by the secret services.[24]

As has been made clear, the power in the land since independence was the army and the generals. Since its commanders were no longer members of the *FLN,* they were not accountable to any political institution whatsoever.[25]

19 Martinez, p 75f.
20 Martinez, pp 94ff.
21 Martinez, p 145.
22 *Chronique des années de sang – Algérie: comment les services secrètes ont manipulé les groupes Islamistes* (*History of the Years of Blood – How the Secret Services manipulated Islamist groups*)
23 He had gained asylum in Germany.
24 *Le Monde,* 25 Sept and *AFP,* 19 Sept 2003 (ANH 05/03 p3).
25 Roberts 2003, p 253, (paper written in 1999).

The *Sécurité militaire* (*SM* – **Military Security**) was formed following French methods; the Soviet KGB and *Stasi*[26] provided assistance and training, and 'a machine to control society without equivalent in the contemporary world was formed.'[27] These men had a mission: 'to eradicate the slightest germ of democracy in order to allow *le pouvoir* to keep on going.'[28]

The *Sécurité militaire* became the **DRS (*Département du renseignement et de la sécurité* – Department of Intelligence and Security)** in 1990, but may still be referred to as the *SM*. Garçon and Affuzi[29] wrote in 1998 that 'apart from the oil and gas sector, the *DRS* is the only institution that truly functions in Algeria, controlling society and an important part of the import/export business, naming top bureaucrats including ambassadors, infiltrating the media, the police, state companies, party politics and armed Islamist groups, suspected of being behind several 'terrorist' attacks, manipulating and misinforming public and presidents...'

General Mohamed Lamari, who became Chief of Staff of the army in April 1993, increased the anti-guerilla corps: its efforts were concentrated on the cities, and Algiers first of all. By eliminating Islamist guerillas ('terrorists'), they left space for the so-called *mujahideen* of armed bands to become 'bosses' of the *communes* who had previously supported the *FIS*.

In many villages, the government often provided people with the means to defend themselves by financing and setting up militias.[30] These became active from the end of 1994. Militias were responsible for many excesses.

---

26   East German secret police.
27   Gèze and Mellah, 2007, p 11.
28   *Reporters sans frontières,* 1996, p 96.
29   José Garçon et Pierre Affuzi, *L'armée algérienne : le pouvoir de l'ombre* , *Pouvoirs*, n° 86, Sept 1998, Seuil, Paris, p. 50, quoted by Gèze and Mellah p 11.
30   Martinez, p 151, notes that the word 'militia' is rejected by the government: 'Whatever certain politicians... may say, there are no militias in Algeria, there are no mercenaries, there are only Algerians, former *Mujahedin*, children of *Mujahedin,* and patriots who have joined the security forces and the Commune Guards to defend the people against murder, robbery and rape.' Martinez describes the militias as the privatisation of violence.

An increase in revenue from international institutions in 1994 made it possible for the military authorities to set up a **Garde communale**[31] to control the reconquered urban areas. The *Garde communale* was accompanied by the feared *Ninjas*, an elite police unit dressed with black hoods like the French parachutists in the War of Independence.[32] They drove everywhere at enormous speed, supported by helicopters, and became synonymous with repression. Torture and mutilation of their supposed opponents was frequent; some fled the country rather than continue such a combat without rules and where everything was permitted: one deserted when he was commanded to kill an injured man who was in hospital. Their *sale boulot* (dirty work) was to destroy, by whatever means, *le mal absolu* of this *sale guerre*. Young men were killed because they were young and therefore considered dangerous. *Ninjas* became the symbol of Algeria's repression.

Each of the groups looked distinctive when not dressed up to represent one of the others. Islamist fighters with flowing beards wore Afghan outfits; the *AIS* wore Cuban-style clothing. The autonomous armed bands in the outskirts of Algiers shaved their heads, put on headbands and did not necessarily have beards. *Ninjas* had black uniforms and hoods. Specialist police in the anti-Islamist struggle wore dark glasses, jeans and trainers with caps back to front, and drove brand-new vehicles.

The DRS would no doubt have argued that it was involved in counter-terrorism, in killing, torturing and 'disappearing' 'terrorists', but as we follow events, it becomes clear that much of it became **state terrorism**: the torturing, 'disappearing' and killing by state personnel of quite innocent civilians.

31   Martinez, p 153f.
32   Catherine Jentile in *Reporters sans frontieres,* p 59f; the name *'ninjas'* demonstrates the humorous ability of Algerians even under unusual conditions, who named them after the heroes of Kung Fu films – but they soon ceased to be a joke.

ALGERIA BANKRUPT; THE POPULATION LIVES IN A STATE OF TERROR

As previously emphasised, since independence in 1962, the Algerian economy had been effectively entirely dependent on oil and gas production. Boumediène incurred the wrath of the French when he nationalised the industry in 1971, depriving France of what was its only significant source of oil and gas. From that time, when production was already increasing, and followed by the 'shock' of OPEC[33] tripling the prices in 1973, the Algerian income from sales of oil and gas rose 'vertiginously'.

Sonatrach became the biggest company in Africa by 1975, employing 120,000 people – the oil and gas division some 10,000[34] – and Algeria had become a major world producer of oil and gas. For some years, it was the fourth largest producer in the world of natural gas, with pipelines carrying gas under the Mediterranean to Sicily and Italy, and to Spain.[35]

Despite the enormous income from oil and gas, Algeria faced bankruptcy in 1994, and politicians worldwide seemed to be agreed that the crisis in the country would be solved economically, not politically. Algerian oil and gas revenues have, since independence in July 1962, accounted for more than 95% of export earnings. As noted earlier, the *FLN* had tried to make agriculture the basis of economic growth, and President Boumediène had concluded that the country must industrialise, particularly into steel manufacture. But under an inert state bureaucracy, a socialist ideology, high costs and the effect of overpowering oil and gas revenues, these efforts were unsuccessful. The country was, and continued to be, suffering

---

33   Organization of Petroleum Exporting Countries. Founded in 1960 to coordinate the petroleum policies and prices of member countries mostly in the Middle East, of which Algeria is one.
34   Malti, 2010.
35   In October 2001, 'Spain imported 75% of its natural gas from Algeria, Portugal (through Spain) 100% and Italy 54%.' (International Crisis Group *Algeria's Economy: The Vicious Circle of Oil and Violence,* 26 Oct 01.)

from what is called the Dutch disease.[36] The finding of large quantities of oil and gas, welcomed by politicians as manna from heaven, can turn out to be a blight on a country's economy. There had been moves away from a socialist to a free-market economy during the Chadli presidency. However, it was the near-bankruptcy of the State in 1994 that precipitated such a drastic change.[37] Algeria had annual oil and gas revenues of some \$9 billion in that year, but the fall in worldwide prices, together with an international debt put at \$26 billion, forced the country to accept outside help. France and the **IMF (International Monetary Fund)** led a behind-the-scenes effort to provide billions of dollars of relief to the country's regime – the French managing director of the IMF, Michel Camdessus, was accused of trying to ram through international funding programmes in order to serve the policy interests of France.[38] This was all highly unusual, but it resulted in the launching of a so-called Structural Adjustment Program. This brought an end to subsidies of such essentials as bread and milk, electricity and gas, and it brought the privatisation of state enterprises and devaluation of the currency. All bad news for ordinary Algerians. But it allowed the regime to gain the upper hand against Islamist armed groups: 'the institution of a market economy was like a method of warfare,' which allowed the 'emirs' of the *GIA* to become part of the (illegal) trading economy, so increasing their funds and capacity for fighting. The *FIS* did not join it and lost out.[39] It might be said that almost overnight Algeria changed from a socialist system to a

36 The term 'Dutch disease' was coined in 1977 by *The Economist* to describe the decline of the manufacturing sector in the Netherlands after the discovery of a large natural gas field in 1959. The term has continued to be used in countries where the economy depends almost entirely on income from oil and gas and where local manufacturing cannot compete with imports. It has a devastating effect on countries such as Algeria, Nigeria and many others (Burgis p 69ff). Wealthy individuals can make millions from it. Burgis describes how, along with the devastating effect it can have on those who live in poverty.
37 ANH, 4/98, p 4: some one million retired people were not going to get their pensions for July 1998 due to lack of cash (report from Algerian radio, 23 Jul 1998).
38 *International Herald Tribune,* 10 Jan 1995.
39 Martinez, p 93.

free market economy, with extraordinary repercussions on the whole of society.[40]

The international financial institutions, and in particular the IMF, thus played a major role in keeping the regime going,[41] but their actions also disrupted existing businesses, and new, highly lucrative business opportunities arose.[42] The privatisation policy that was introduced in 1994 was taken over by participants to their own advantage – the economy became a 'plunder' economy.[43] The intervention was a trump card in the government's war against the Islamist armed groups. Neither side succeeding in winning, but the financial windfall from the IMF allowed the build-up of repressive 'anti-terrorist' operations, increasing the number of men from 15,000 in 1993 to 80,000 in 1996.[44]

It was small businesses and those living below the poverty line who bore the brunt: the price of milk, bread and other necessities of life increased dramatically and the Algerian dinar was devalued by 40%. Petty traders – grocers, bakers and others – tried to retain a business in a market economy which was new to them: they faced extortion from armed groups and repression from the security forces. Bigger fish were military entrepreneurs who flourished and made big money from 'import-export' of such commodities as pharmaceuticals, stolen cars and drugs from businesses such as hotels in Algeria and France, and from land which had been handed over to them at independence in recognition of their war efforts.[45]

Djamel Zitouni's *GIA* destroyed and burned down unproductive companies in deficit which the government no longer wished to fund. Workers were suddenly made redundant, without the state having to announce redundancies, thus

---

40   Yasmina Khadra, who describes the insecurity in Algiers in the 1990s in *Double blanc (a crime novel)*, has one of the characters say that in business there is only one practice of faith: 'to turn a profit'.

41   Martinez, p 228.

42   Martinez, p 119.

43   Martinez, in referring to 'the plunder economy', quotes J-F Bayart, S Ellis and B Hibou 1997 on Africa: *La criminalisation de l'Etat en Afrique*.

44   Aggoun & Rivoire, p 379.

45   Martinez, p 24.

avoiding confrontation with the workers and economising on the intervention of the police in the face of demonstrations.[46]

The code of success was fending for oneself, swindling and violence.[47] An informal economy, or black market, called **trabendo**, which had been present for years, could not only increasingly flourish but be controlled by the state.[48] Military entrepreneurs set up networks of *trabendistes* – young people of the neighbourhood who had gone around Europe since the mid-1980s to bring back consumer goods which could then be resold in Algeria at great profit. The entrepreneurs could provide foreign currency and distribution networks, and they could also obtain import permits. Informal trade was originally controlled by influential people in the state, but it gradually came to form a 'parallel economy' to that of the state.[49]

Meanwhile, the state sector was being destroyed not only by armed groups – 45,000 workers lost their jobs[50] – but also by privatisation:[51] every closure or privatisation of a factory threw tens or hundreds into complete despair. Acts of sabotage on state enterprises, such as transport, pharmaceutical and cement manufacturing, aimed at weakening the regime, benefited the private sector who replaced it, bringing fat profits to 'new' operators.[52] Business was arranged for friends and relatives – this went back to the 1980s, if not earlier: war was a means of accumulating wealth and prestige.

Most of the Algerian population lived in a state of abject terror. It is impossible to give more than a brief idea of the varying conditions across the country in cities, towns, suburbs and villages. For those trying to lead as normal a life as possible, this depended on where they saw the balance of power. In the

46 Samraoui, 2003, p 8.
47 Martinez, p 51.
48 Martinez, p 25.
49 Martinez, p 25, note 16, quotes A Henni: *Qui à légalisé quel trabendo?: Peuples méditerranéens 52-53 1991.*
50 Aggoun & Rivoire, p 378, quoting Martinez: *A qui profite la guerre? Politique internationale 79, printemps 1998.*
51 Martinez, p 120ff and p 217.
52 Martinez, pp 122-3.

cities, the presence of security forces and 'emirs' meant that criminals could prosper. Armed groups would seek supplies in villages to keep them going in the *maquis*: civilian militia groups (*Groupes de légitime défense*)[53] set up to fight them or to defend the village could have absolute control of life and death.

Moving about the country was fraught with danger, both for civilians and security forces. Death and worse had to be faced on the roads. Road blocks marked off the respective spaces of armed groups and security forces, but armed groups were reported as dressed as security forces and security forces as armed Islamists. Fearful road users would not know by whom they were being stopped, and many innocent civilians, including busloads of people, lost their lives. Women, both at road blocks and elsewhere, were at high risk: rape followed by death was only too frequent, but it is impossible for the western world to understand how rape victims who did survive became complete outcasts of society. The honour of the family had been desecrated by the act, for which the victim was somehow held responsible and banished, to become homeless, destitute and often condemned to a brothel; abortion is banned in Algeria.[54]

People stopped using cafes where there would be informers; being afraid of arrest, they stayed all day at home in front of the television. This could cause such overcrowding that brothers and sisters would take shifts using the same bed – three eight-hour shifts in twenty-four hours.[55] On a housing estate in a suburb of Algiers overlooking the Mediterranean, where the parents slept in the only bedroom, Ghania Mouffok[56] described how seven brothers and sisters – one at least unemployed since the age of nineteen – somehow slept in the living room. In other flats,

---

53 They were also known as 'patriots'.

54 According to a report in the Algerian newspaper *Le Matin* (23 May 2000), more than 8,000 women had been raped 'by armed groups' since 1991, and it was estimated that 3,000 children were born as a result (ANH May/Jun 2000).

55 Martinez pp 76-78.

56 In *Reporters sans frontières* p 15f; the building described was built as a temporary solution by the French under the 1956 'Constantine Plan' for 'Muslim populations' living in *bidonvilles*.

children slept on the kitchen floor or on the ground floor in what were supposed to be toilets. These families supported the *FIS*.

By late 1998, it was reported[57] that 40% of the population was living below the poverty threshold, that begging was found not only in the cities but in small villages, that there was an average of 7.4 persons per dwelling – one of the highest rates in the world due to lack of housing; drinking water would be distributed in Algiers on one day in three, but for how many hours per day? The price of milk, Djilliale said, had increased by ten times in a few years, and many could not afford it for their children. *Le pouvoir* did not seem to be conscious of the situation.

Following *FIS* control of *communes* in Greater Algiers after they had won local elections in 1990, at which time people had lived safely, a military campaign was launched to take them back. A policy of terror was initiated in April 1993:[58] torture, humiliation, deadly reprisals, enforced disappearances. On the Mitidja, the plain outside Algiers where poor suburbs had sprouted, the civilian population was under a state of double siege: armed bands inside controlled by 'emirs', who could not leave because the army, who checked everyone entering or leaving, encircled it outside. There was a policy of 'let them rot' on the part of the military, and these *communes* became ghettos. Les Eucalyptus, a dozen or so kilometres south of Algiers, went from euphoria under *FIS* councillors to the 'hell' of civil war. The social work and control of crime under the *FIS* ended; extortion, crime and protection rackets plagued petty traders, and the local population had to provide for the needs of both the army and the armed groups. 'A visit by soldiers to a trader in broad daylight could be a prelude to his murder by armed Islamist groups.'[59] The wealthier people had long ago taken flight. One of the results of all this was the emigration of 450,000 Algerians to France between independence in 1962 and 1982.[60]

57 Djillale Hadjasj, *Le Monde Diplomatique*, Sept 1998.

58 Martinez p 22.

59 Martinez p 73f.

60 From *L'Immigration algérienne en France* by Gérard Noiriel. The Algerian population in France in 1982 was 800,000. It will have greatly increased since then.

Young men faced national service with the army and at the same time Islamist groups needed to replenish their ranks. A 'strategy of terror' was implemented to 'encourage' them to join the Islamists: the death threat hung over those who did not. When one son was called up for military service, some families chose that the second son join the Islamists: a sort of hope that one might survive.

The plight of those facing a different 'hell' is illustrated by the reports of two Algerian newspapers[61] early in 1999. These illustrated all too graphically the destitution of peasants and families who had fled from the countryside to the towns, and to a society they did not know. B Grissi reported that behind a facade of well-being, Oran hid an increasing pauperisation: 'nothing can depict the reality of a breakneck descent to hell which nothing seems able to stop.' A photograph showed children 'for sale':[62] the child leaves home in a second, never to return; the parents are far from insensitive and said that "it's better than suffering from our poverty." Young people only thought of amassing enough money to leave for distant places – there was no other work in a place like Chlef, west of Algiers, which used to have 50,000 inhabitants and where industries had been closed.

The Algerian elite lived, and continue to live, on the heights and slopes above the city of Algiers in suburbs such as the pleasant pinewood suburbs of Hydra, where I lived in 1962-5.[63] These were also the favoured areas for foreign embassies and their staff. To the west of Algiers is the *Club des pins*, a highly desirable pine-forested area developed by the French as an exclusive club on the Mediterranean,[64] and now a fortress where

---

61   *La Tribune*, 21 Jan 1999 and *Liberté*, 9 Febr 1999.

62   ANH Jan/Feb 1999 (quoted from *La Tribune*, 21 Jan 1999 & *Liberté, 9 Feb 1999* – *Liberté* included a photo of three tiny children on a pavement).

63   One of the most notorious torture centres was (is?) in Hydra where I lived in the early 1960s. I, of course, had no idea that this also existed under the French in the War of Independence while I was resident there.

64   I had been invited to this delightful spot in 1962. Much later, a new elite was provided with villas at 'derisory rates', only to be ousted by Chadli. In 1993, it became a camp entrenched behind barbed wire, 'completely cut off from an Algeria which was tearing itself apart and which they were supposed to be governing.' (Ghania Mouffok in *Reporters sans frontières*, p 19.)

thousands of individuals live, 'to whom everything is permitted, which is above the law... protected by the all-powerful *DRS*...' Outside of these idyllic spaces more than 30 million people are deprived of their most elementary rights.'[65]

A NEW PRESIDENT; A PEACE AGREEMENT SCUTTLED; BOMBS IN PARIS[66]

The *Haut Comité d'État,* installed after the cancellation of the January 1992 elections, appointed **Liamine Zeroual** as **president** for a transition period of three years in January 1994. Almost immediately he announced a 'dialogue for all', and although there were positive moves towards consensus, the violence intensified and opposition to Zeroual became apparent within the regime only too quickly, the division between 'conciliateurs'– which included Zeroual – and 'éradicateurs' surfacing repeatedly.[67] Zeroual was a man of integrity, well placed and sympathetic for dialogue with the *FIS*; he had fought in the War of Independence but had not been a member of the French military, and had not been involved in the army's decision to depose Chadli, interrupt the election process, ban the *FIS*, and so on. He was thus ideally placed for dialogue with the *FIS*, but he had to reckon with the opposition of many of his military colleagues, and that of France; he made a start by replacing some, but it proved too much for him.

Liamine Zeroual was Head of State during the period of the most terrible violence of the 1990s. Hundreds of Algerian citizens were being killed each week. I shall look at a small number of what are perhaps the key events of the period; much has come to light since then. There has never been any official investigation, nor has anyone, to my knowledge, been charged or convicted of any of the killings or enforced disappearances or been found responsible for any of the appalling torture which took place at that time, or since.

65   Aggoun & Rivoire, 2005, p 596.
66   ANH, 20 Jan 1995: *Libération* and *El Pais,* 14 Jan 1995.
67   Roberts, 2003, p 151f.

It had been suggested that President Zeroual was having talks with the *FIS* leaders Madani and Benhadj in November 1994[68] but these came to an end. On the other hand, an event in Rome in late 1994 and January 1995 proved that dialogue was possible: it might even have brought the violence in Algeria to an end. **The Catholic Sant'Egidio community,** based in **Rome,** which had been successful in bringing peace to Mozambique, arranged a meeting of representatives of all major Algerian political parties, including the *FIS, FLN* and *FFS,* which between them had obtained 83% of the votes in the December 1991 elections; only the '*eradicateur*' parties refused to attend. The military government was invited but the Interior Minister described the Rome talks as meddling by 'retarded politicians' and the government rejected the plan 'totally and in detail'[69]. On 13 January 1995, an agreed statement (*contrat national*)[70] was made, calling on the government to avert a civil war, calling for a political and peaceful solution to the Algerian crisis and engaging the signatories to respect a number of principles, including:

- the rejection of violence to attain or maintain power
- the rejection of any type of dictatorship
- respect for human rights
- the release of all political prisoners
- the army to be kept out of political affairs.

The generals were put in an almost impossible position: how to reject the agreement without giving the impression that the regime was a dictatorship. Nevertheless, they rejected the agreement 'globally and in detail'. They had to convince world opinion that the Islamists were monsters and that they were the

---

68   *El Pais,* 09 Nov 94.

69   ANH, from the *Independent* 16, 17 and 19 Jan 1994.

70   ANH, Dec 94-mid Jan 95 (From *Libération* and *El Pais,* 14 Jan 1995; there was relatively little in the British press but Roberts 2003 (p 181, footnote 19) states that an English translation of the full text of the Platform (the *contrat national*) was published in *Mideast Mirror* in London 16 Jan 1995.

first line of defence of the West in facing up to the peril of hordes of Islamists.[71] Ali Belhadj, No 2 in the *FIS* and under house arrest, declared that he was satisfied with the *accords de Rome,* but that they risked inciting the *'éradicateurs'* to take action in Europe to torpedo them: how right he was. Madani was more reticent. European governments, including France, appeared to give some lukewarm support to the Rome proposals, as did the European Union, but did little to push for anything more concrete to be done. An extraordinary opportunity was missed, never to be repeated, but *le pouvoir* was adamantly against it.

Roberts[72] notes that the process showed that the political parties took a responsible statesmanlike view of the crisis; the *FIS* agreed to reject violence, to call for an end to exactions and attacks against civilians and foreigners, and to end the destruction of public property. The *FIS* also accepted the democratic principles of 'political pluralism' and 'alternation of power through universal suffrage'. The Platform was, writes Roberts, a remarkable piece of statesmanship, offering Algiers and Paris an honourable way out with minimal loss of face. The US State Department warmly welcomed it, but the British response was non-committal, just 'noting' it. French officials made vague positive noises, but the way this was done gave no real support to the Platform and did nothing to assist the various sides to come together. Roberts states that a change in French policy could have allowed France to recover the goodwill of the Algerians and also secure its own interests in the long term.[73]

The response of Algiers was furious. So came to an end, at what turned out to be a relatively early and crucial stage of the violence, the best possibility for a peaceful solution – and this was before the violence crossed the Mediterranean to France.[74] When dialogue failed, a presidential election was held in January

---

71 Malti, 2010, p 299.
72 2003, p 172ff.
73 Roberts, 2003, p 160ff.
74 Hocine Malti wrote that if the Sant' Egidio initiative had gone ahead it could have saved tens of thousands of lives. Algeria-Watch, 10 Jan 2015, http://www.algeria-watch.org/fr/aw/malti_fin_de_regne.htm

1995. Zeroual won it and it was described as 'formally more democratic than almost all presidential elections in the region.'[75]

It was while the talks were going on in Rome that an **Air France Airbus**, with 241 passengers and crew on board, was **hijacked** on 24 December 1994 at Algiers Airport by four Algerians dressed in the uniform of airport employees; three persons, including an Algerian policeman, were killed. After a dramatic couple of days it was stormed by French elite forces in Marseille on 26 December; 1,000 to 1,500 shots were fired. The four who exploded two grenades were killed; ten *gendarmes* were injured, but all the hostages were safe and slid down two emergency chutes.[76] Questions had arisen: how could the four hijackers have got into the plane with arms and explosives? Why did the Algerian authorities refuse to take part in a judicial inquiry? Were they putting pressure on France at the time of the Rome talks?[77]

Sheik Abdel-Baki Sahraoui, eighty-five, a co-founder of the *FIS*, Imam and Rector of the Paris mosque, was assassinated in his mosque on 11 July 1995. This was regarded as a warning to *FIS* leaders, especially those outside Algeria, to all Algerian opposition that supported dialogue, and to France.[78] He was the proof that there were moderates among the Islamist leaders with whom it was possible to have a dialogue; he had understood the true nature of the eradicators and of the *GIA* and had become an embarrassment both to the Algerian generals[79] and to Charles Pasqua, France's Minister of the Interior, whose strategy was to demonise the *FIS*. Who was responsible for the Sheik's death?

The Algerian newspaper *La Tribune*[80] printed an article claiming that the killing of the Imam would be followed by other attacks: many details were given. Whereas *La Tribune* claimed

---

75   Roberts, 2003, p 319.
76   *Le Figaro;* article twenty years after the event: http://www.lefigaro.fr/assets/
      marignane
77   Aggoun and Rivoire, 2004, p 414f; Laribi, p 153ff, provides extraordinary details.
78   Jean-Paul Mari in *Le Nouvel Observateur,* 20 Jul.
79   Aggoun & Rivoire, p 445.
80   17 Jul 1995.

that its source was Islamist, the French police were convinced that the source was the Algerian military security.[81] Be that as it may, a **bomb** eight days later **in a Central Paris RER Metro train** at St Michel station caused seven deaths and injured eighty-five, and on 17 August, a bomb in a rubbish bin near the Arc de Triomphe caused seventeen injuries. On 27 August, an unexploded bomb was found on the TGV railway line north of Lyon. The French authorities were at first very careful not to blame Algerian Islamists. Other bombs followed and the French identified the Algerians as directly responsible for the attacks in France; in July 2002, Khaled Nezzar, questioned about the 1995 attacks and whether there were links between the *GIA* and the Algerian *DRS*, said that the French services had known what was going on and they could answer this question.

Many years after the bombs, witnesses gave accounts of what had happened.[82] Ali Touchent, an Algerian in France, had agreed early in 1993 to work for the Algerian *DRS*: his job was to infiltrate the European Islamist milieu on behalf of the *DRS,* and he was named leader of the *GIA* in Europe in April 1995. Abdelkader Tigha said after he defected that information obtained by Touchent was passed to European intelligence services so that active Islamists in Europe were arrested. Young Islamists were sent from Algeria by the *DRS* and by Djamel Zitouni, *DRS* head of the *GIA*. The network thus organised by the *DRS* and Touchent was responsible for the bombs in France.

The attacks were not only catastrophic for the *FIS*, but also for Alain Juppé, the French Prime Minister, who was in favour of the Rome Platform, and put in an impossible position. Systematically presented by the press as the work of Islamist groups (the *GIA*) and therefore of the *FIS* who had supported the Rome Platform, the French had at the same time to support the Algerian generals who were fighting the Islamists. Interestingly, Charles Pasqua, who was so anti-*FIS*, said that the attacks must have been organised by the *DRS* since the Islamist groups were

---

81   *Nouvel Observateur,* 03 Aug 1995.
82   Aggoun & Rivoire, pp 451-459.

incapable of funding that type of operation. But how could the French government distance itself from the generals while French people were dying or injured almost weekly in attacks reputed to be the work of extremist Algerian fanatics? Following the bombing, no French official ever criticised the Algerian regime.

Fourteen years after the event, the question of who was responsible for the bombings was 'settled' in October 2009. Rachid Ramda was found guilty at the Special Court of Assizes in Paris, on appeal, of providing the means and having given the orders for the bombings; all arguments for the defence were brushed aside, there were very serious gaps in the prosecution's evidence, of which the magistrates showed themselves aware,[83] but the result was that the file on the bombings was closed for good. The French press took almost no notice, but then, as Algeria-Watch asked: *Who cares?*[84]

MONKS KILLED[85] AND HUNDREDS OF CIVILIANS MASSACRED

Early in 1996, France was again traumatised. On the night of 26/27 March, seven French Trappist monks aged fifty to eighty were abducted from the Cistercian monastery of Tibhirine, some 60 km southwest of Algiers on the edge of the Atlas Mountains; only the severed heads were later recovered. This area had been a stronghold of maquis Islamists since 1992, and the monks had been under pressure to leave, but they had worked with the local population since 1933 and refused to give up their life-long vocation of solidarity with the poor, in which Christians, Muslims and Jews could live together in mutual respect.[86] Their relationship with local people seems to have

83 The Advocate General did recognise that the *DRS* had manipulated and organised the *GIA*, but said there was no point in going back into history.
84 Pascal   Tourion,   http://www.algeria-watch.de/fr/article/just/attentats_paris/ramda_verdict_sans_surprise.htm, 10 Nov 2009.
85 *Le Monde,* 20, 27 Apr & 30 May 1996.
86 Evans & Phillips, p 226.

been quite remarkable, and they gave succour and medical help daily to whomever needed it – including members of the *GIA*. A dramatic and sensitive film *Des hommes et des dieux* (*Of Gods and Men*), which won many prizes, was produced in 2010; it reopened the question of the assassinations.

It was perhaps not unexpected when the **Archbishop of Oran**, outspoken in his advocacy of tolerance and Catholic-Muslim dialogue, was also murdered under strangely suspicious circumstances in August 1996.[87] The Archbishop of Algiers said that priests and the religious were targets in Algeria,[88] but no more than the Algerian population among whom they were working. In a communiqué published in the Saudi *El Hayat* on 26 April, the *GIA* claimed responsibility for the abduction; like many other communiqués attributed to the *GIA,* there were immediate questions as to its authenticity. There were, as in so many of these atrocities, conflicting reports and many unanswered questions.

Extraordinary stories began to emerge. A group of dissident officers (*MAOL, Mouvement algérien des officiers libres*), based in Madrid, made horrific allegations – through the internet – about senior generals, but *MAOL* did not reveal their identity and doubts arose. The spokesman for the group said that the Algerian drama "reveals manipulation that goes beyond any fiction."[89] Others followed in writing of Tibhirine and later massacres and of their likely authors.

In 2003, Abdelkader Tigha[90] stated that the objective of the abduction of the monks was to poison international opinion, and particularly opinion in France, so that it would not weaken in the face of 'Islamist barbarism'. The monks had to disappear, as would Djamel Zitouni, who had kidnapped them.[91] He was

---

87 Aggoun & Rivoire, p 489f.

88 Other priests and religious people had already been killed.

89 *Le Monde,* 26 Nov 1999 (http://www.algeria-watch.org/mrv/mrvreve/maol5.htm), Y.B. and Samy Mouhoubi write that it is impossible to be sure that the revelations of the *MAOL* Spokesman, Colonel 'B. Ali', are true but it is impossible to ignore them. This article is horrifying. I have included little of their reports.

90 *Le Monde,* 10 Dec 2003, *Risques internationaux* 15 Dec 03.

91 Evans and Phillips p 231, quoting *Libération* 23 Dec 2002.

replaced as leader of the *GIA* by Abou Talha Antar Zouabri, another *DRS* man.

Thirteen years after the assassinations, the evidence presented before a French investigating judge by General François Buchwalter, who had been French military attaché in Algeria at the time, was made public.[92] He suggested that it may have been the Algerian authorities, and not Islamists, who assassinated the Archbishop of Oran two months later, because he had embarrassing information on the monks' fate. For this and so much else, the need for proper inquests was reinforced.[93] The French were, and still are,[94] as much alarmed by the prospect of a public inquiry as the Algerian authorities. When the statements became public, President Sarkozy decided to lift French state secrecy and called on the Algerian authorities to reopen their own investigation, saying, "Relations between great countries must be built on truth, not lies." Articles, books and TV programmes appeared over many years concerning what happened at Tibhirine, and it has to be concluded that without doubt the *DRS* was responsible.[95]

Gèze and others have explained[96] that, contrary to all other foreign countries, inquests by the French authorities into deaths and injuries of French citizens in Algeria have never taken place. They say that there is only one explanation: since 1962, Algiers has never been, to Paris, a foreign capital like the rest and, never wanting to face up to the terrible truths of 132 years of colonisation

---

92   *Libération, 7 Jul 2009.*
93   Amnesty International MDE28/23/97, Nov 1997. 28/36/97 (with distressing photos) stated that people were blowtorched.

   Lahouari Addi (Algeria-Watch, 29 Jul 2009) asks how Algerian institutions, such as the DRS, the police and the gendarmerie – whose job it is to protect the population – can have the confidence of Algerians when there has been no inquest or investigation into Tibhirine and later massacres such as those in Bentalha and Rais.
94   2016.
95   Moines de Tibhirine : http://www.algeria-watch.org/fr/article/just/moines/geze_puissance_desinformation.htm
96   This article had appeared in *Le Monde* on 23 Apr 2013 (http//www.lemonde.fr/idees/article/2013/05/29/tibehirine-la-france-passive-face-aux-derives-du-regime_3420453_3232.html), signed by fifteen writers and others. The article also states that between September 1993 and August 1996, no less than thirty-eight French nationals were assassinated in Algeria, mostly attributed to the *GIA*, but in no case was there any inquest at the time.

and the Algerian War of Independence, both the political left and the political right in France have chosen to close their eyes to the authoritarian nature of the Algerian *pouvoir*. The very close collaboration between the French authorities (the *DST*) and the Algerian security forces (the *DRS*) has led to the *de facto* support by Paris of the war conducted by *le pouvoir* against the civil population and the 'Islamists'. In 2009, Alain Marsaud, a former deputy in Sarkozy's government, was reported as saying that "both Paris and Algeria had conspired to 'bury' the truth and that the French government had been 'terrified' of the authorities in Algeria."[97]

Massacres of hundreds of civilians in small towns just outside Algiers shocked the world in late 1997. Shot and burned alive in their homes, children and babies thrown off balconies, people blowtorched, burnt alive, decapitated, and pregnant women disembowelled.[98] These places had been strongholds of the *FIS*, and 'terrorist' Islamist groups were immediately said to be responsible. But many troubling questions arose, just as quickly, which cast doubt on the official explanations. Why, in the most militarised part of the country, did no one intervene to stop the massacres, which often lasted several hours and took place only a few hundred metres away from army and security forces' barracks and outposts? Survivors and neighbours told Amnesty of telephoning or running to nearby security posts seeking help, with the security forces there refusing to intervene. One survivor said, "The army and the security forces were right there; they heard and saw everything and did nothing... They waited for the terrorists to finish their dirty task and then they let them leave."[99]

Some years after the massacre at **Bentalha**, which had taken place on the night of 22/23 September 1997, Nesroulah Yous, non-commissioned officer in the *DRS*, published his dreadful eyewitness account of the assault on the village by a group of 200

97   John Lichfield, the *Independent*, 9 Jul 2009.
98   Amnesty International – MDE28/36/97, 'Algeria, A Human Rights Crisis' described massacres in three villages.
99   Amnesty International MDE28/36/97.

assailants.[100] He said, "At the time I did not want to believe in the army's guilt, because I had a tendency to think that this was Islamist propaganda," but it became clear that the army played an active role in both the preparation and the carrying out of the killing, including:[101]

- ambulances and armoured vehicles remained stationary the whole night, under the surveillance of the military, at some tens of metres from the massacres that were going on – they barred the way to those who wanted to come in and rescue the inhabitants of the *quartier*
- an army helicopter was flying over the scene the whole night
- in the middle of the night, powerful lights in a field went on and were then turned off as if to light the attackers' way
- the assailants exploded dozens of homemade bombs, each of more than 30 kilos, brought there in trucks
- the assailants were allowed to stroll out of Bentalha and escape down a main road, the security forces making no attempt to intercept them, although well placed to do so
- some ten days before the drama, soldiers had ordered the caretaker of the local cemetery to dig some thirty graves, which would be used to bury victims.

The book caused a furore in France. At the time, wrote François Gèze,[102] it was 'obscene' to imagine that some top army officers of an internationally respected state could plan, in cold blood, the assassination of hundreds of their compatriots. But the sincerity and the details provided by Yous left no doubt; there

---

100   *Qui a tué à Bentalha? 2000.* This book rapidly became out of print and I could not obtain a copy at the time I was writing this.
101   Abstracted from Gèze, 2000 and Roberts, 2003, p 309.
102   Gèze, Yous and Mellah, *Algérie, un témoignage terrifiant,* 2000.

was a foundation for this hypothesis. Roberts[103] wrote that although Yous was convinced that the assailants actually were a special army commando or death squad, he could not prove this. However, 'Yous's testimony provides the basis of a *prima facie* case for the charge of complicity (of the army), as accessories, before and after the fact, in mass murder.' Still, for many, there is nothing to understand about this barbarity except that it was the insanity to which religious fundamentalism can lead – the view that had been continually expressed by the international media, and particularly by the French.

Abdelkader Tigha provided explanations for some of what Yous recorded. He said that the *CTRI*[104] in Blida, where he had worked as a non-commissioned officer for the *DRS* and which was one of their principal torture and extrajudiciary execution centres,[105] called *la machine de mort*,[106] had assisted the *GIA* to enter these villages and

---

103   Roberts, 2003, p 310.
104   *Centre territorial de recherche et d'investigation,* Department for Information and Security.
105   Algeria-Watch, 2003. *Algérie: la machine de mort,* p 28.
106   *La machine de mort* not only describes in horrific detail the means of torture, largely based on the techniques used by the French during the War of Independence. It provides details of the secret centres of detention – some one hundred of them – in nearly all of which detainees were systematically tortured and died, or were executed. Evidence comes from ex-members of the security forces – both military and police, from Algerian human rights lawyers, from organisations such as AI, Human Rights Watch and the *Fédération internationale des ligues des droits de l'homme* and from a variety of other publications and witnesses. The care with which the work has been carried out leaves little room for doubt as to what has been going on. The authorities have not denied torture and mistreatment but claim that they were simply cases which got out of control, and that this was necessary in the fight against 'terrorism'.
    The following description is from the 1995 Amnesty International Annual Report:
    The dramatic increase in torture which began in 1992 continued. Methods of torture most commonly cited were: the 'chiffon' (cloth), whereby the detainee is tied to a bench and a cloth soaked with chemicals or dirty water is forced into the mouth; burning using a blowtorch (*chalumeau*); electric shocks to the ears, genitals and other sensitive parts of the body; tying a thread around the penis and progressively tightening the thread; sexual abuse using bottles and sticks; beatings; and death threats and mock executions. Drilling holes in the back, feet or legs was also reportedly used as a method of torture. The authorities failed to investigate a single torture allegation, to Amnesty International's knowledge. The AI Secretary General, in New York, publicly demonstrated the use of a blowtorch against individuals.

towns, and had given instructions to the army and security forces not to intervene if the villages were attacked.

Following one of the massacres, Kofi Annan, Secretary General of the United Nations, called for 'an urgent solution', saying that "we are in the presence of a situation which for a long time has been regarded as an Algerian problem. It is extremely difficult for us to act as though nothing was going on... and as though we should just abandon the Algerian population."[107] In New York, the Algerian Permanent Representative lobbied intensely against Kofi Annan and obtained an assurance that the UN would not get involved any further on the issue of Algerian massacres. The UN and European Parliament delegates were allowed to visit Algeria in 1998, but they were not permitted to go to any of the 1997 massacre sites.[108]

Further personal disclosures had come with the sensational publication of Habib Souaïdia's *La sale guerre*[109] (*The Dirty War*) in 2001. At the age of sixteen he was profoundly patriotic and only wanted to serve his country. He became a second lieutenant in the Algerian army in the early 1990s, but what he saw and had to do became so abhorrent to him that he sought refuge in France. It is a deeply moving and distressing account of the manipulations by the generals, and especially of Mohamed Lamari. Souaïdia wrote: 'I have seen my colleagues set fire to a boy of *fifteen*, who burned like a living torch. I have seen soldiers slaughtering civilians and blaming "the terrorists". I have seen senior officers murdering in cold blood simple people who were

---

107 Aggoun & Rivoire p 506-7.

108 *Le Monde* 23 Feb and 23 Jul 98.

109 Souaïdia, Habib, 2001. *La sale guerre. Editions La Découverte.* Souaïdia's accounts have been seriously questioned by Mohamed Sifaoui, 2014, who uses the term 'false testimony'. It had been intended that Sifaoui would assist, together with François Gèze, in the preparation of *La sale guerre* but this cooperation ended by Géze suing Sifaoui. (*http://www.algeria-watch.org/farticle/sale_guerre/sifaoui_diffamation.htm Communiqué de presse: François Gèze, directeur général des Éditions La Découverte, assigne en diffamation le journaliste Mohamed Sifaoui*) Despite this, I have chosen to quote from and note some of what Sifaoui has written in what follows. This gives a sufficiently different opinion, which demonstrates the difficulty of being quite sure about the truth.

suspected of Islamic activities. I have seen officers torturing Islamic activists to death. I have seen too many things. I cannot remain silent. These are sufficient reasons for breaking my silence.'

Not all of the army was culpable: there were many honest and upright officers – who, he suggests, did not obtain advancement. The war was led by elite units: the special services of the army, the *DRS* and key units of the police and *gendarmerie*. He knew, he says, that certain *GIA* groups were directly manipulated by the 'special services', even though the groups may not have realised this; he was convinced that the massacres were premeditated and that the generals were behind them,[110] just as they had been in massacres in which he had assisted where the number of dead was much less. An Algerian officer who has given the order to kill twenty innocent civilians can easily give the order to massacre a village.[111]

Souaïdia says[112] that there were two wars going on: one, which he was willing to serve in, was to destroy the armed groups; the other, in which he was not willing to serve, was targeting civilians. Those suspected of Islamist sympathies were systematically arrested, tortured, killed. The *DRS* attributed the atrocities and killings that they had carried out to the Islamist groups; at the same time they manipulated armed groups from within. The dirty war was a secret war: there were no written instructions within the special forces. There was also, he says, a psychological war going on: how many Islamist sympathisers are left in the country today?

The main problem in Algeria, Souaïdia wrote, was not religion or Islam – it was, and it still is, injustice. 'If an end is put to the injustice, peace will come to Algeria. Therefore it is necessary to stop the corrupt individuals who are continuing to rob the huge assets of the Algerian people.'[113]

---

110 Souaïdia, 2001 p 304.
111 *Idem,* p 306.
112 *Idem,* p 313f.
113 Keenan in *State Crime Research*, 8 Jul 2015.

General Khaled Nezzar sued Souaïdia for libel in a long high-profile case in a Paris court in 2002. Nezzar lost his case.[114] As the years have gone by, other writing[115] has affirmed the status of Habib Souaïdia's testimony and the criminal roles of the Algerian regime, its army and the *DRS*.[116]

For Yasmina Khadra,[117] one of Algeria's most celebrated novelists, who was a senior military officer and had taken part in combat operations, the army could do no wrong. He portrays a professional army locked in battle with savage 'terrorists' and guilty of only a few 'isolated' crimes. His books (including the most popular, *Morituri,* which illuminates the darkest corners of Algeria's underworld and is devoted to the quite reasonable theory that things are never what they seem in Algeria) are found in all Algerian bookshops, but Habib Souaïdia's book *La sale guerre,* and Nesroulah Yous's *Qui a tué à Bentalha?* are banned. In *Wolf Dreams*, Khadra follows the army's official explanation for its failure to prevent massacres like the one in Bentalha: 'Too cumbersome: the military betray their presence from the outset, and always arrive too late.'

Eighteen years after the so-called 'Berber Spring' of 1980, the singer **Lounès Matoub**, idol of the young, was killed. His songs made him no friends with either Islamists or the regime,

---

114 Mohamed Sifaoui (*Histoire secrète de l'Algérie independante* 2014 p 172-4) has written highly critically of the activity of the *DRS* and *le pouvoir* (what Sifaoui calls *le système*) but is even more critical of Habib Souaïdia, whom he accuses of clearing the Islamists of their crimes, imputing nearly all of the massacres and crimes committed in the 1990s to the Algerian authorities and pretending that the armed groups were the creation of the secret services. Sifaoui himself (2004 p 341-2) appeared as a witness for Khaled Nezzar and writes that he had always denounced the Islamists, was favourable in January 1992 to the electoral process being stopped, but that he also denounced the authoritarianism of the regime and called for democracy in the country. He said in court that he rendered hommage to Nezzar for having stopped the electoral process and for having prevented the Islamists making Algeria another Afghanistan but that he would never agree to the politics that had been followed in Algeria since 1962.

115 Including, in English, *An Inquiry into the Algerian Massacres*, Editors: Youcef Bedjaoui, Abbas Aroua and Meziane Ait-Larbi. Hoggar Press, 1999, 1473 pages, with a Foreword by Eric Avebury.

116 Eg. Keenan, 2009.

117 He adopted a woman's name (his wife's) in order to avoid military censorship. Three of his books, including *Morituri*, have been translated into English.

but he became enormously popular in his native Kabylia. He defended two causes: the Berber culture and secularism, and he had two adversaries: *le pouvoir* and Islamist fundamentalists.[118] On 25 June 1998, he was killed; demonstrations and rioting went on for weeks. Years later, two men were arbitrarily arrested; one admitted under torture that he was the killer of Matoub, but after ten years in prison still no criminal case had been brought.[119]

FROM GIA TO GSPC (1998)

Bentalha and Raïs were by no means the only massacres in the mid and late-1990s. In an extraordinary revelation in March 2006, Prime Minister Ahmed Ouyahia revealed that a massacre had killed 1,000 people and three villages had been entirely destroyed at Ramka and Had Chekala in the west of the country; the earlier official figure had been 150 killed. "We hid the truth," he said, "because one doesn't direct a battle while sounding the bugle of defeat."[120] The *GIA* was on all occasions held responsible by the government and the media, and had become notorious for the terror that it had sown between 1993 and 1997. Following the massacres, more and more voices were raised, asking what had really been going on, and calls by human rights organisations multiplied for an independent international enquiry.

Mohammed Samraoui says that he was a direct witness, as early as the first months of 1991, to the fact that the 'deciders' were manipulating radical Islamists in order to discredit the *FIS*.[121] The *GIA* was gradually infiltrated by the *DRS*, who

---

118 Jacques Amalric, *Libération*, 26 or 27/28 Jun.

119 AW, 3 Jun 06 & Christophe Ayad, *Libération, 22 Mar 2008.*

120 *El Watan,* 22 Mar 2006; more was made clear and many more questions asked by Algeria-Watch ten years later (4 *Jan* 2016) http://www.algeria-watch.org/fr/aw/massacres_relizane.htm

121 Samraoui, 2003b, p 75ff. He describes in detail what he eventually understood the *DRS* were doing, for example, the setting up of a 'false' Islamist group in the Kabyle Mountains, in conjunction with one of the leaders of the *MIA*, a small Islamist group.

controlled it completely by 1995.[122] But then it no longer served its purpose, and *le pouvoir*, 'Tewfik', and Smaïl Lamari, the numbers 1 and 2 of the *DRS* since September 1990, needed to be rid of it. The *GIA* had served various complementary functions: terrorising the population who in the early 1990s were supporting the Islamist opposition; providing a substitute for the 'true' Islamist opposition – the *AIS* – thus discrediting it and provoking internal dissensions; justifying 'total war' against civilians and forcing them to accept draconian antisocial measures; providing the reason for international support of the Algerian regime.[123] Gèze and Mellah, quoting Samraouï,[124] write that the *DRS* had infiltrated the *GIA* as early as September 1992 and took control of it at the end of 1995; the international call for an enquiry into massacres in late 1997 meant that the *GIA* had to go.

In the autumn of 1998, the formation of the **GSPC Groupe salafiste pour la prédication et le combat** was announced. It was formed by Hassan Hattab[125] and it attacked only military and militia targets, unlike other armed groups, who were said to behave just like bandits. The *GSPC* was at first active only in Kabylia (an area where Islamists had very limited support) and only attacked military targets and led few attacks. But it increased its attacks on civilians and foreigners, and it in turn was seen to have become an instrument of the *DRS*.

Abdelkader Hachani, No 3 of the *FIS*, who had led the party during the elections of December 1991 while the two leaders (Madani and Benhadj) were in prison, was assassinated on 22 November 1999 in the waiting room of his dentist in the centre of Algiers.[126] He had also been imprisoned and since his release in October 1997 had continually been under police escort. He

---

122 Gèze and Mellah, *Al Qaida au Maghreb, ou la très* étrange *histoire du GSPC algérien*, p 2007.
123 Gèze and Mellah, *idem* p 10. Algeria-Watch, 22 Sept 2007.
124 2003b: *Chronique des années de sang.*
125 Hassan Hattab was also an agent of the *DRS* (Géze 2013: http://www.algeriawatch. org/pdf/pdf_fr/geze_jeu_trouble_regime_algerien.pdf)
126 *Le Monde,* 24 Nov 1999.

can be regarded as the man responsible for the success of the *FIS* at the 1991 elections, and after his release from prison he was an important conciliator behind the scenes within the *FIS* and in supporting Zeroual's peace efforts.[127] He did not correspond to the Islamist stereotype: he was extraordinarily courteous, opposed to the Islamist armed groups and was apparently the pet hate of the militant in this process.[128]

In France, G Grandguillaume wrote in 1995[129] that: 'One explanation is now present in all minds: it is Islamism that has led Algeria into the decay in which we see it today.' To what extent did this view, misleading and dangerous as it was and is, affect the policies of western countries towards Algeria?

LANGUAGE AND RULE OF LAW

In early July 1998, it had been announced that all conferences, TV emissions and so on must be translated into Arabic, whereas French was the language of most of the more highly educated of the population and of business. Akram Belkaïd[130] has more recently written that there are two national languages: Algerian Arabic and *Tamazight,* or Berber; Algerian Arabic is a colloquial form of Arabic and the language spoken by most of the population.

The result of this Arabisation policy was in part responsible for what Roberts describes as an acute identity crisis.[131] He saw this as part of the catalyst for the terrible violence that engulfed Algeria; he placed the responsibility on the Chadli regime in using the cultural question as a diversion from the regime's disastrous mishandling of social and economic issues. Tassadit Yacine, in an interview with José Garçon[132] stated that the authorities, instead

127 http://www.algeria-watch.org/fr/aw/assassinat_hachani.htm
128 *Le Monde,* 24 Nov 1999.
129 Quoted in Martinez, p 1.
130 Belkaid, 2005, p 92.
131 Roberts, 2003, p 138ff (paper written in 1993).
132 *Libération,* 6 Jul 1998 (ANH 4/98 p 3).

of pushing Algerian society towards harmony, have – especially at times of crisis – tried to exploit these differences in order to pitch Algerians against one another. The regime could then pose as arbitrator in the name of safeguarding 'national unity'.

Despite four written constitutions in a short space of time, Algeria has **no rule of law** and hence human, civil, political, socio-economic and cultural rights are at the mercy of arbitrary rule and abuses of authority.[133] Security forces shot young people like dogs, took them away, tortured and disappeared them. Rule of law implies that every citizen is subject to the law, including lawmakers themselves. 'Only the advent of genuinely representative and law-bound government in Algeria itself can constitute a progressive outcome to the terrible drama of the country.'[134] He says that the revolt of young people in Kabylia denouncing *'le pouvoir assassin'* and demanding *'l'état de droit'* gives rise to a degree of optimism: 'Only the Algerians themselves can be the architects of this development if it is to be genuine and durable. The rest of us can only help.'

For most of the media in France, the cause of the violence was quite clear: it was caused by the mix of Islam, Islamism and genocidal terrorism.[135] However, the mission of the military since 1995 'to liquidate the AIS and *FIS*' had largely been attained, and

---

133 Roberts, 2003, p 107f.

 In 2005, Roberts said, when giving evidence to the British Parliament about political issues and developments in Algeria (http://www.publications.parliament. uk/pa/cm200405/cmselect/cmfaff/36/5020105.htm), that "the lack of rule of law arises out of the fact that the Algerian state is not a state bound by law (*un* état *de droit*), but (is) characterised rather by a high degree of arbitrariness at every level of authority. This fact is partly a legacy of the revolutionary manner in which the state was constituted by the historic *FLN* in 1962, but it is above all a consequence of the excessive weight of the executive branch of the state and the correspondingly stunted powers of the legislature and the dependent nature of the judiciary."

134 Roberts 2003 p 200ff. Roberts told me that he did not understand why Amnesty International and other human rights organisations do not call on governments, such as that in Algeria, to account and call for the introduction of a legally binding rule of law.

135 The violence for numerous observers was a 'horror without precedence' and could only be compared with Nazism or the *Khmer Rouge*, but Gèze writes that there was the weight of tradition of violence by the French since 1830 and by the generals since the war of liberation.

the level of violence in the country should have been reduced –
but that still did not happen for some years. Little by little, the
question had arisen as to whether the *GIA* was a creation of the
DRS.

An elite of chiefs of the *DRS*, of generals and ministers and
others (who nearly all lived at the protected *Club des pins*), the
more important of whom did not go out except in armoured
vehicles, had accumulated colossal fortunes in Switzerland
and elsewhere and was ready to do everything to protect its
privileges. They had already started to kill one another in 1993:
on 21 August, Kasdi Merbah, the head of the *DRS*, despite his
armoured vehicle 'was assassinated with a professionalism that
made the official hypothesis that it was an action of Islamist
terrorists totally improbable.'[136] Merbah had at the time been
engaged in negotiations with the *FIS*. President Zéroual and
his advisor Mohamed Betchine, who had been behind the
truce with the AIS in October 1997 and were in favour of an
agreement with the *FIS*, were up against Mohamed Lamari,
head of the army, and 'Tewfik' of the *DRS,* who were ready to
go to any lengths in eradicating it. During the summer of 1998,
there was a public battle between the two clans in the Algerian
press, where every newspaper title was supported by one or
other. This was followed by the resignation of President Zéroual
on 11 September 1998. At the same time, as always happened
when the struggle worsened, massacres took place again.

---

136 Gèze: *Algérie, un témoignage terrifiant,* 2000.

5

THE TRAGEDY OF THE 'DISAPPEARED'

I was much involved for some twenty years in the crime of 'enforced disappearances', or simply 'disappearances', in Algeria. When carried out by police or security forces, it is generally called counter-terrorism, but when extrajudicial killings, torture and disappearance are carried out by the state to the extent that they were in Algeria, it seems clear that this was **state terrorism**. Tens of thousands of people, many of them *FIS* members and their relatives, including women and young people, neighbours and friends, were arrested by security forces in raids and searches, and most were probably then dreadfully tortured; many were no doubt summarily executed. These, we believed in Amnesty, were carried out both by armed groups – about whom we learned nothing – and the security forces – about whom we learned only too much. Around 3,000 very detailed dossiers were compiled by AI in the years up to 1999 concerning individuals that the organisation had learned about and many more after that date, all of whom had been arrested by police or state officials.[1] Most of these people had been

---

1   Those taken by armed groups were not heard of again.

taken away, at night or even during the day, from their homes in the presence of relatives, colleagues in workplaces and local inhabitants in the street. This was done by members of the local *gendarmerie* and others, often armed, but who didn't produce any arrest warrant. Often the police were known personally to the families, who were informed that their relative was being taken for a routine control, or for questioning, and that they would be freed very rapidly.[2] Many of these families, when they heard nothing, spared no effort to try and get news from the authorities: in the few cases where a reply was forthcoming, they were told that the disappeared person was not known to the authorities, had run off to join an armed group or had been abducted or perhaps killed by an armed group. But of their whereabouts the authorities denied any knowledge. The men – and the few women – who disappeared came from every social class, political background and walk of life, from cities and rural areas, were rich and poor, and many were members of the *FIS*.

It became clear that the Algerian so-called 'struggle against terrorism' was based on techniques devised by the French during the Algerian War of Independence. It was a 'death machine',[3] planned by generals of the *DRS*. Torture became a way to crush the individual's dignity, his honour, his faith and his humanity. General 'Tewfik', Head of the *DRS* since 1992, was the principal organiser of the strategy in Algeria. Islamist armed groups were also responsible for terrible crimes against civilians but in Amnesty we never learned of any disappearances carried out by them who could be identified, perhaps because there were none – all victims were killed.[4]

Why were innocent people so dreadfully tortured in independent Algeria? It was rarely to gain information, which had probably been the main object of the French earlier. It was to terrorise the man, his family and those close to him, to obtain confessions, most often false, justifying what was being done, and

2   Amnesty International 1999, p 11; see also Amnesty International 2009.
3   *Sidhoum, Salah-Eddine* and AW *La machine de mort, oct 2003.*
4   This was the supposition in the head office.

to destroy them, physically or psychologically and to strike fear among the population. It may be helpful to quote the Amnesty researcher for Morocco in 1991: "Disappearance is used not just to eliminate from the scene people against whom the state has no sustainable legal charges, but it is meant to create an atmosphere of fear which spreads throughout the country. For the family of the victim, disappearance may be a greater punishment than execution: death ends the matter, grief heals, life resumes. Since the authorities never admit to holding a 'disappeared' prisoner, the family do not know what has happened and whether their relative is alive or dead."[5] Grief, and the inability to know what happened, continues.

Learning the truth and obtaining justice for families is at the heart of work done by NGOs on the crime of enforced disappearance – when a person is arrested or kidnapped and is never heard of again. It is a particularly heart-rending crime. Wives, husbands, brothers and other family survivors of disappearances do not know what has happened to their relative. Where the disappeared person is the breadwinner in the family – and this of course is usually the case – the family may have no income and have the greatest difficulty to find enough to live on, to send children to school and to lead any sort of normal life. This is added to the immense trauma of the absence of a loved one. The police who arrested them in their homes, at their work, in the street, were often known to the families, but once arrested it was quite exceptional if anything was ever seen or heard of them again. Years after thousands disappeared in Algeria in the 1990s, the authorities recognised that some 5,000 had disappeared, 'kidnapped', they said, by armed partisans, or they had rejoined the maquis Islamistes.[6] The figure of 18,000 was advanced in 2005.[7]

5   Power p 198.
6   Nassera Dutour: *L'insoutenable lucidité d'une mère. Debbih, Abdelkrim, La Presse, Actuel, 7 Mar 2002*.
7   By LADDH. A more plausible figure say Gèze and Mellah in *Le Monde, 16 May 2005*. http://www.lemonde.fr/idees/article/2005/05/16/la-sale-guerre-en-algerie-responsables-et-coupables-par-francois-geze-et-salima-mellah_650231_3232.html.

Nassera Dutour, living in Paris, was phoned from Algiers to say that her second son, Amine, aged twenty-one, living with his grandmother in Baraki, Algiers, who had gone out to do some shopping, had been arrested on 30 January 1997[8] by three police officers in suit and tie according to witnesses, and had not been seen again.[9] Nassera immediately went to Algiers and tried to get information about his disappearance from all the various authorities – by going to barracks, police and others, with no success whatsoever. She knocked on doors and crossed the country and she found many mothers and their husbands who had suffered the same fate; she decided to gather them together and by herself to break down the wall of silence about disappearances. "Keeping quiet about such injustice is to be complicit with the assassins of my son. Amine, my son, does not merit that."[10]

Despite families going to barracks, police and other authorities, Nassera quickly realised that they could do little in Algeria, where they were met by silence and by the contempt and scorn of the authorities. She therefore set out to seek international help from foreign[11] governments and organisations. But families were very worried at the idea: they still had other sons or brothers who were not safe from being disappeared themselves. Coming together, however, gave them confidence and, organised through Amnesty and others, Nassera and a number of mothers (and a couple of fathers) visited Geneva, London, Paris, Brussels and Amsterdam in July-August 1998. They had a list of just 130 families at that time and used the slogan *Vous avez pris nos*

8   There had been an attack on the Wali, the governor of Algiers, and disappearances continued for three days.

9   http://www.la-croix.com/Monde/Avec-Nassera-Dutour-la-memoire-des-disparus-d-Algerie-2012-05-04-802418 Some of what I have written about disappearances is what I remember Nassera telling me, and some is taken from a large amount of material I received personally from her. Disappearances and other atrocities continued until at least 2008 and occasionally later than this.

10   She has no legal right under the Algerian family code, adopted only in 1987, to do this. Only the father is the legal guardian.

11   These notes are from an article *Bilan de dix ans d'action des familles de disparus* (Assessment of ten years of Action by Families of the Disappeared) by Nassera in *Courier de l'ACAT (action des chrétiens pour l'abolition de la torture)* Sept-Oct 2008.

enfants vivants; vous nous rendez nos enfants vivants. (You took our children alive; return them to us alive.) They were interviewed by the British press in London at the AI International Secretariat office and we took them, led by Donatella, to meet the Foreign Secretary and others in the Foreign Office, and to Parliament to meet government and opposition MPs and Lords in the all-Party Parliamentary Committee on Human Rights.

Aided by Amnesty, Oxfam (NOVIB), *FIDH* and other French NGOs and families resident in France,[12] Nassera set up the *CFDA (Collectif des familles de disparu(e)s en Algérie* – Group of Families of the Disappeared in Algeria) in Paris in 1998, where she had lived for many years, to make people aware of the magnitude of the human rights crisis in Algeria and to call for the release of the 'disappeared' from prison. She had very little in the way of office facilities and no experience of computers, so we arranged that AI groups working in Britain on Algerian cases came together to buy a computer for her. It was then taken out to Paris by an expert from the International Secretariat, who set it up and taught Nassera how to use it. She has been quite extraordinarily active in many ways for more than twenty years, as almost any of her quarterly newsletters, of which for many years I provided an English translation, demonstrate.

Within Algeria itself, despite threats and intimidation, Nassera gathered together mothers, fathers and relatives whose sons or husbands had disappeared, and set up a twin group to *CFDA* in 2001 in Algiers, called *SOS disparus*, run for many years by her mother. *SOS disparus* and its offices[13] have been very active but have somehow survived despite government edicts prohibiting such work, and never having been recognised.[14]

---

12   And with the support of various French NGOs. Nassera has also received major support from a Catalan NGO: *Fonds Catalan pour la coopération et le développement,* from *NOVIB the Catholic Committee against hunger* and from others.

13   In Algiers, Oran and elsewhere.

14   Is it perhaps because Nassera and her work has become so well known internationally and through the Algerian press? I have also often wondered how she can apparently visit Algeria so easily from Paris.

Following the example of mothers of the Plaza de Mayo in Buenos Aires, Nassera organised weekly and annual demonstrations in the centre of Algiers and elsewhere, which have continued until today. There are frequent lectures, meetings and discussions. Nassera has also been involved in an extraordinary number of other actions, seminars, debates, conferences, contacts with the media and frequent training courses to do with human rights and work of all kinds in Algeria, France and elsewhere.[15] She has actively assisted other human rights NGOs working in Africa and the Mediterranean area.[16] She has been, and continues to be, very active, and has become known worldwide for her work; she has been awarded a number of international prizes, including the Oscar Romero prize in 2011.[17]

With Nassera's determination, *SOS disparus* has continued to work in Algeria, visiting families, tracking down mothers and others of disappeared people in their homes and gradually meeting and gathering together over years the most detailed evidence of thousands of disappearance cases.[18] Indefatigable in her drive to know what happened to her son, and for truth and justice for the families and for the disappeared, she has said that "I go wherever I can find an attentive ear; I haunt the United Nations in New York and the Human Rights Commission in Geneva..." "One day I met a representative of a public authority in Algeria – he advised me to stop, otherwise I risked rejoining my son."[19]

---

15 See, for example, 'Training and seminars' http://www.algerie-disparus.org/nos-actions/formations/
16 Including, for example, the African Commission on Human and Peoples' Rights (*CADHP*).
17 Nassera came, with the lawyer Moustapha Bouchachi and a young representative of *Le Rassemblement Action Jeunesse (RAJ)*, to speak at a most inspiring AIUK AGM at Warwick University.
18 A most moving book, *Devoir de mémoire*, A Biography of Disappearance, Algeria 1992, Omar D. Published by Autograph ABP, London 2007. It is a book of photographs of some twenty persons who disappeared from various towns and villages, their families, their usually very humble homes and adjacent scenes.
19 Nassera Dutour: *L'insoutenable lucidité d'une mère. Debbih, Abdelkrim, La Presse, Actuel, 7 Mar 2002.* http://www.algeria-watch.org/mrv/mrvdisp/dutour_espoir.htm

Nassera has very frequently visited the Working Group on Enforced or Involuntary Disappearances (WGEID) at the United Nations in Geneva, each time to take more details of Algerian disappeared persons and to press for action. The WGEID published a major report when it had received 477 documented cases of enforced disappearance: three were women. Many were middle class and the profile 'is clearly incompatible with young guerrilla fighters acting clandestinely.' The military, the police, the *gendarmerie* and the security forces were said to be responsible, and they often acted with civilians or militia.[20] Some of the individuals reported responsible could be named by the complainant, and in many of the cases, the arrest was witnessed by others. More and more families overcame their fear and reported disappearances, forcing the issue to be debated in parliament, on the street and on the front pages of the national press. AI stated that this was a major breakthrough since nobody could say: "I did not know."[21]

One of the results of the continual pressure brought by Nassera and *SOS disparus* on the Algerian government over the years was that Farouk Ksentini, President of the *CNCPPDH*,[22] officially the government's leading human rights defender, after years of doing nothing carried out an investigation into disappearances. He said[23] that he thought there had been 7,000 to 10,000 disappearances, maybe as many as 12,000. He submitted his report to the President on 31 March 2005 and gave interviews to the media in which he stated: "These disappearances certainly occurred and are the work of people acting on behalf of state bodies." However, he added that the state is "responsible but not guilty."[24] The report was understood to have been sent to the

---

20 Government 'self-defence' groups.
21 AI report MDE 28/04/99 dated 3 Mar 1999.
22 National Consultative Commission for the Protection and Promotion of Human Rights. Nassera seemed to be almost weekly in Farouk's office during several years in attempts to get action on disappearances.
23 Human Rights Watch: Time for Reckoning: Enforced Disappearances and Abductions in Algeria. Feb 2003, Vol 15, No 2.
24 AW 04 Apr 2005 http://www.algeria-watch.org/en/hr/aw_ksentini.htm.

President, but it was never heard of again nor published – it too disappeared.

Following the promulgation of the Charter for Peace and National Reconciliation,[25] which was voted in by a large majority of the population in 2006, Nassera and *SOS disparus* were told that Article 46 of the Charter had solved the problem and nobody was permitted to make complaints about state officials: all *CFDA*'s cases were dismissed. Meaningful investigations within Algeria became impossible, as did enquiry into actions of the state and the military and the violence of the radical Islamists. To raise these matters became a criminal act which could lead to imprisonment and/or fines. Not only did the Charter not provide any solace whatsoever for families of the disappeared, but Article 46 forbade them raising the matter.[26] M Ksentini[27] told families – after many years of investigation by his commission – to calm their hearts and spirits and forget what had happened, in order to turn the page on a most sad event in the country's history. M Ksentini stated that the files were now closed and nobody had the right to talk further about the matter. At a later stage, the government tried to bribe families of disappeared by offering cash if they would sign that their relatives were dead;[28] many did so since they lived in abject poverty. But none of this stopped Nassera and *SOS disparus* from continuing to strive for truth and justice.

---

25 See Chapter 7.

26 Not only did it do this, but it rendered anybody who denounced the authors of violations liable to imprisonment. Alkarama 30 Aug 2016 http://fr.alkarama. org/item/2032-algerie-comme-un-feu-qui-ne-s-eteint-pas-le-deni-du-droit-a-la-verite-et-a-la-justice-des-familles-de-disparus. Alkarama is a Swiss-based organisation, established in 2004, to assist all those in the Arab World subjected to, or at risk of, extrajudicial killings, disappearances, torture and arbitrary detention.

27 The *CNCPPDH* would now 'disappear': *disparu* is the extraordinary word used by Ksentini in reply to questions from Achira Mammeri (TSA 1 Jun 2016 http://www. algeria-watch.org/fr/mrv/mrvrap/creation_conseil_dh.htm): Ksentini said that it would be replaced by a *Conseil national des droits de l'Homme* (CDH), a National Human Rights Council. Ksentini said that this was being done because the *CNCPPDH* was responsible to the President; the CDH would be known to be at the service of the nation and not a governmental institution. I have heard nothing further of it.

28 They had to sign a statement that the disappeared person was dead, some that he was a terrorist.

Disappearances, torture and state killings carried out by the state are 'crimes against humanity'.

Families continued to demonstrate weekly, and also on other annual dates such as each 29 September, anniversary of the 'Charter for Peace and Reconciliation' and to show the authorities that their fight for truth and justice continued. At their demonstration in September 2018, *SOS disparus* had called for this to take place at *la grande poste*,[29] a prominent and significant building from French times, but the police, who had been patrolling the area before the demonstration, very rapidly dispersed it.[30] On 10 December 2018, the 70th anniversary of the Universal Declaration of Human Rights, participants were treated violently, taken to commissariats, questioned, and phones confiscated; they were released in the afternoon.[31]

Nassera has now been trying, through all means possible – the Algerian state, the **United Nations** and others, to obtain truth and justice for the disappeared and families… She has frequently visited the Working Group on Forced Disappearances (WGFD) at the United Nations in Geneva to take more lists of Algerian disappeared persons and to press for more action. The UN, not just the WGFD, has issued reports condemning individual disappearances and other human rights abuses inflicted by the Algerian government. In 2014, writing about cases of disappearances submitted by Nassera at that time, the UN Commission on Human Rights recognised that, for the 25th time, the Algerian State had violated the International Pact relating to Civil and Political Rights.[32] But these conclusions, though welcome, can be, and seem to be, just ignored by the Algerian government. However, in the event that anyone suspected of crimes against humanity is charged, this information held by the UN will be invaluable.

29   The main Post Office.
30   *CFDA* Newsletter Sept 2018.
31   I give these only as examples of what happened at so many demonstrations over the years.
32   http://www.algeria-watch.org/pdf/pdf_fr/cfda_16juin.pdf

Once again, I can only stress how remarkable Nassera's efforts have been. Marwan Andaloussi wrote in 2018 that 'the drama of the disappeared... was an absolute taboo for the Algerian press for a dozen years and if it had not been for the courageous combat of families, who assembled every Wednesday in Algiers under police truncheons, the question of the disappeared would have been removed from the collective memory.' [33]

33   La presse algérienne, vraiment libre? Liberté https://algeria-watch.org/?p=64323

6

WHO RULES ALGERIA? 'LE POUVOIR'

The Algerian street has long spoken of *le pouvoir*. But what, and who, is *le pouvoir*? 'Nobody really knows how the Algerian regime functions.' This was written in 1995[1] and, although we now know the names of most of the generals behind *le pouvoir*, the statement remained true for years. Who takes the decisions? Who decides? By means of what mechanism? It is as if running a country is the same as running a war – there is the same need for secrecy: all is 'opaque'. Since January 1992, the President and government – in a country where there is no rule of law and no democracy – have been puppets operating at the behest of a group of generals who never appear in public and who are unknown to the outside world. Liamine Zeroual, who was President from 1995 to 1999, had some power deriving from the group of 'conciliator' generals, but the difficulties that Abdelaziz Bouteflika had when *le pouvoir* chose him to be President in 1999 demonstrated even more clearly the chronic weakness of the Presidency of the Republic. The army, despite having the power, does not govern: it delegates

---

1   *Reporters sans frontières*, 1995, p 63 and 65f.

its business of governing to civilians with little power:[2] a prime minister, ministers and parliament – who may be vetoed by *le pouvoir*. It is with these ministers that ambassadors and their staff from other governments must deal; it has three dictatorial traits: it is authoritarian, it has confiscated all powers and it controls the entire population. On the other hand, the face that it turns to the outside world is much more attractive than that of dictators.

José Garçon wrote[3] that it is the army – the *ANP* – together with the security forces, who exercise the real power, based on shifting clans. The power of the army is not shared, except with the security forces – the only institution to function without rivalry between different services. It spreads its net over society, controlling an important part of overseas business, appointing government officials, infiltrating political parties and armed Islamist groups who are suspected of being behind various assassinations, deliberately misinforming public opinion. If the security forces are formally dependent on the army, the state of war has allowed them to extend their fields of action so that nobody really knows who controls whom. An Algerian diplomat has said that 'the security forces are masters in the art of confusion and mixing the true and false, which allows *le pouvoir* to put forward motives which can mask some shameful purposes.' For thirty years, the army and security forces pulled the strings behind the *FLN*, dividing and smashing opposition. This allowed the 'deciders' to continue in power whatever the price. It has also permitted them to play cleverly in friendly countries, especially France. Altaf Choudja[4] writes that the army is not a simple instrument at the service of the state; it is the State and it renders no account to anybody.

In 1998, Labat[5] asked: "Do you know any other country whose real chief is unknown?" Do you know the names of the twenty generals who run the country? She could name four at that time.[6] We know, she said, that there are many clans and

---

2   Roberts, 2003, p 266.
3   *Libération*, 4 Jun 1997; ANH 3/97 p 3.
4   *Reporters sans frontières*, p 66.
5   Middle East, Jun 1998; from ANH 3/98 p 1.
6   Zeroual, Betchine, 'Tewfik', and Nezzar, 'who is supposed to run the show'.

that they were formed in many different military academies with opposing ideologies in France, the USA, Syria, Egypt and the Soviet Union. The important factions were two groups, one of which had fought in the War of Independence against France and had received training in military academies in Egypt, Jordan and Iraq – and included President Zeroual – and the second consisted of those whose careers had started in the French army and who later deserted to the National Liberation Army (*ALN*).[7] The only thing that we know is that they meet in full caucus and take their decisions unanimously, but there are suspicions that officers are also settling accounts within the military establishment. This is why the question is raised: who is killing whom? What is at stake is the control of the $11 bn oil revenue per year. But there are only rumours in this country.

It was only in 2001, following the testimony of Hichem Aboud, an ex-officer of the Algerian military security and a refugee in Paris, that the names of eleven generals were published: nine had been non-commissioned officers in the French army who joined the Algerian army (*ALN*) between 1958 and 1961.[8] The following names come up most frequently in this account:

- **Mohamed Mediène, called 'Tewfik'** (or 'Toufik'), Head of the *DRS* – Military Security
- **Smaïn Lamari**, Head of Counter-espionage and No 2 in the *DRS*
- **Khaled Nezzar**, officially retired, had been Chief of Staff and Minister of Defence
- **Larbi Belkheir,** became Director of President Bouteflika's Cabinet
- **Mohamed Lamari,** Chief of Staff (Head of the army).

7   Roberts, 2003, p 271ff .
8   Farid Aïchoune & Jean-Baptiste Naudet in *Le Nouvel Observateur,* 19 Jun 2001 from ANH 03/01.

Only 'Tewfik' and Smaïn Lamari did not serve in the French army. According to the article, these eleven 'deciders' choose the ministers, *walis* and directors of the most important public businesses. There were generals for each of the major imported products, *trabendo* (corruption) having become the No. 1 Algerian activity. But, the article said, there are generals and others who have nothing but their salaries; 'the army is not totally rotten.' Akram Belkaïd[9] says that the worst thing about *le pouvoir* 'is that public opinion is convinced that it is always in control of events,' whereas, he writes, its strategies most frequently lead to catastrophes which in turn lead to new means of trying to repair the situation – but which continues to get worse; it is more than likely that the October 1988 riots were provoked by one of the clans of *le pouvoir* using them to take precedence over another clan. *Le pouvoir* supported the Islamists at that time in order to scare civil society and demonstrate that it (*le pouvoir*) was the sole alternative to the *FIS*; although the generals are known as the *décideurs*, they rarely merit this term: they are more 'non-deciders', whose obsession is always to gain time.

A horrific statement, which Mohammed Samraoui[10] says remains engraved in his memory, was made only three months after the January 1992 military putsch. Smaïn Lamari, No. 2 in the secret service, said in the presence of numerous officers: "I am ready, and decided, to eliminate three million Algerians if this is necessary to maintain the order that the Islamists menace." There can be difficulty in distinguishing where counter-terrorism becomes state terrorism, but there can be no doubt that *le pouvoir* in its acts of torture, disappearance among the civilian population and manipulation of Islamists to carry out massacres of villagers, was guilty of state terrorism.

Before 1991, the President of the country, a military man, was also the head of the single ruling party, the *FLN*, a position that gave him real power. Since the military putsch, however, as has been made abundantly clear, the real power has lain

---

9   Akram Belkaïd, 2005, p 22ff.
10   *Chronique des années de sang,* p 162.

with *le pouvoir*, a group of generals who never publicly make themselves known.[11]

There is a centuries-old tradition of resistance to the state which makes the Algerian people highly suspicious of their rulers; clandestine resistance means that decisions from on high are as often as not just a basis for discussion, if taken note of at all. This is at the heart of the problem of the Algerian bureaucracy.[12] Political parties in Algeria are not political in a Western sense: they are rooted in the cultural sphere – Arabo-Muslim, Islamist or Berberist – so that they do not have nationwide support. This means that they are unable to hold the government to account.[13]

The Algerian electorate had been called on to vote four times between November 1995 and October 1997. The first had led to the election of Liamine Zeroual as President of the Republic; this was followed by a referendum on revision of the constitution and by parliamentary and local elections. Roberts has analysed these,[14] which were, he says, evaluated by the West in terms of whether or not they were 'democratic'. Roberts points out that, like the French before them, Western commentators were unable to grasp that Algerian society functioned in accordance with different rules.[15] The elections were held in order to resolve

---

11   Mohamed Sifaoui p 27ff, writes that the nature of the power of the Algerian secret services and *le pouvoir* can only be understood by going back to the early years of the War of Independence, when the duo *FLN/ALN* was located in eastern Morocco. Abdelhafid Boussouf became the 'strong man' of *wilaya* V there and began organising a real 'war machine'; the importance of security forces and the need for information was recognised and Boussouf became known as 'the father of the Algerian secret services'.

12   Roberts, 2003, p 113.

13   Roberts, 2003, p 264.

14   Roberts, 2003, p191ff (paper written in Nov 1997); he is in no doubt that although 'a serious amount of rigging occurred,' ... in the legislative elections of Jun 1997 (p 194)... 'the available evidence suggests that a broadly pre-determined result had been secured.' (p 195)

15   Tunisia, which remained an Ottoman province until French rule in 1881-3, had experienced an Ottoman modernising movement from the 1820s, when constitutionalism was a central theme of Arab and Middle Eastern politics. Algeria missed out on this opportunity and was influenced only by French concepts of politics (Roberts, 2003, p 207-8).

political problems and the question asked should perhaps have been as to whether they did so, not whether they were 'democratic'.[16] They allowed some sort of formal constitutional legitimacy to return.

The *FLN* was set up to fight the War of Independence and grew out of that to become the one-party government of the country for nearly thirty years. However, since 1962, it has been the army which is the principal locus of power – the 'party', the *FLN* – had to explain the decisions taken elsewhere, but it was not its business to reason why; there were only two points of doctrine: the imperative of achieving and safeguarding the sovereignty of the Algerian state, and the imperative of achieving and thereafter preserving the unity of the Algerian nation. Everything else was open to debate and negotiable.[17] This in part explains why the *FLN* has never split but instead has splintered: we have seen this in the behaviour of Prime Minister Hamrouche, who bolstered the *FIS*'s electoral appeal while sabotaging his own party – the *FLN* – in 1989-90. In these circumstances, there is great difficulty in developing political parties and hence in developing a democratic system of government. It is in part because of this difficulty that Islamists can argue that Western conceptions of democracy are inappropriate to Algeria.[18]

The **RND (*Rassemblement national démocratique*)**, a right-wing party, was formed by President Zeroual in order to counter the *FLN* in 1997 under rather curious conditions which need not detain us. Its Secretary-General, Ahmed Ouyahia, a Kabyle, was Prime Minister for some twelve years between 1995 and 2012. He is considered to be part of the 'eradicator' clan. He was not popular and claimed that many of those who had disappeared at the hands of the security forces had belonged to terrorist groups, a statement that international human rights organisations questioned. However, he is credited with

---

16 A point made to Roberts by an Algerian academic in the immediate aftermath of the elections (2003, p 192).
17 Roberts, 2003, p 109.
18 Roberts, 2003, p 115.

mediating a long-standing dispute between Kabyle leaders and the government.

The *FIS* (*Front islamique du salut*) had won elections and was banned in 1992, but its lack of visibility since the 1990s deserves explanation. Roberts explains convincingly[19] why support for it diminished after its success at the local elections in 1990 – it was already much less successful in the December 1991 elections. The *FIS*, he says, based its populist strategy on the assumption – which was quite wrong – that '*le peuple est musulman au fond.*' ('The people are Muslim at heart.') It assumed that Algerians could be won easily to the religious Islamist cause; they were won to the *FIS*, but not to the world view of radical Islamism. This cause came from the Middle East but was not related to Algerian Islam and had not been Algerianised by an Algerian thinker. It was an ideological import, which was not suitable for Algeria in the 1990s.

The *FIS*, despite its harsh rhetoric about *les voleurs*[20] and so on, worked within the constitution and dealt with the *FLN*, whose objective, supported by the Algerian people, was to meld Algeria into a nation state. This was an entirely opposed aim to that of radical Islamists who wish to establish an Islamic state and therefore, Roberts concludes, it has always been unreasonable to suppose that the Algerian Islamists would ever come to power in their own right. This is not a view that has been held by the French and Western media.

Labat concluded in 1998[21] that the Islamists would be defeated but that many of the conservative points of the *FIS* programme – although not of the revolutionary elements – had already been implemented.

In 1989, the Chadli government had been deliberately encouraging the formation of parties which were canvassing diametrically opposed, and quite irreconcilable, conceptions of the state. There were three main alternatives to the *FLN*: the

---

19   Roberts, 2003, p 98ff.
20   'Thieves' – describing those in power who amassed vast sums through corruption.
21   *Middle East,* Jun 1998.

FIS based on *Shari'a* law, the **RCD (*Rassemblement pour la culture et la démocratie*)** and its Berber socialist rival, the **FFS.** The last two both stood for a secularist constitution of the state which would be unacceptable to most Algerians – but not to the Berbers of Kabylia, nor the Francophile middle class. The two Berber parties, the FFS and the RCD, both of whom found some support outside Kabylia, were, and remain, opposed to each other; the former had always been supportive of the *FIS*, while the RCD virulently opposed it and supported the line taken by the 'eradicators'. In addition to these parties, there was a plethora of small parties, including the Communist party and three Islamist parties,[22] all three of which are non-violent, accept the constitution of the state and claim to accept modern democratic norms. Only one, the **MRN**,[23] has consistently opposed the government.

Hocine Aït Ahmed, the leader of the FFS, was a hero of the War of Independence, and one of the few *chef historiques* who survived. He had been arrested in 1964 and sentenced to death but escaped from prison in 1966. He chose exile in Switzerland with occasional visits to Algeria: he was a remarkable leader of the FFS, a fierce opponent of the Algerian regime and highly respected internationally. He had been an indefatigable fighter since 1992 for a pluralist political solution in Algeria, and had been one of six candidates for the presidency of Algeria in 1999 – all of whom resigned the day before the election, citing serious fraud. Aït Ahmed died in 2015.[24] He had asked, in 2004, fifty years after the start of the War of Independence, "What remains of the dreams of freedom, dignity, progress and justice which were at the origin of our wonderful expectations in November 1954?"[25]

---

22 Roberts, 2005: 'The legal Islamist parties are offshoots of the Egyptian Muslim Brotherhood.'

23 The Movement for National Reform. (*Harakat al-Islah al-Watani; Mouvement de Reforme Nationale*, MRN)

24 Aït Ahmed died in Lausanne; his body was taken back to be buried in his natal village in Kabylia. Hundreds of thousands of people – perhaps even more than a million – were at the village and lined the roads as the cortege passed by. 'He was regarded as our Nelson Mandela.' (*El Watan* 04 Feb 2016 and 26 Dec 2015.)

25 ANH, Sep/Oct 2004.

The state of emergency, which had come into force on 9 February 1992, had allowed the government to arrest some 10,000 Islamist, or supposed Islamist, sympathisers and militants who were imprisoned in the Sahara for years, under conditions which can only be imagined. It allowed the government to penalise any speech deemed threatening to the state or public order, to ban public meetings, marches and demonstrations and it has more generally allowed *le pouvoir* to tighten its complete control of events. Roberts wrote[26] much later that 'The violence that has ravaged Algeria since 1992 has... confirmed the ascendancy of the military in Algerian political life and the weakness of all civilian forms of politics... The civilian leaders of the Islamist movement were almost entirely outflanked by the Islamist armed movements and, within the regime, the army's General Staff and intelligence chiefs became the main source of decision making... (S)uccessive presidents proved entirely unable to impose their authority.'[27]

Television and radio had been strictly controlled by the State until *Al Jazeera,* which set up in Qatar in 1996 to broadcast across the Arab-speaking world.[28] It employed ex-BBC staff who had been in Saudi Arabia until the station there was closed down by the Saudis and it was for years a beacon of light across the whole Arab world;[29] the only one not subject to censorship, and broadcasting freely.[30] In June 2004, Prime Minister Ouyahia called it 'a channel whose sole aim is to tarnish Algeria's image.'[31]

---

26 Roberts, May 2007, *Demilitarising Algeria*, p 1. Carnegie Endowment for International Peace.
27 Much later, President Bouteflika, backed by his powerful military clan, had some authority.
28 And later to other language areas, including English. It was watched with much interest by many of us.
29 It broadcast in what is called Standard Arabic, which is similar to classical Arabic, in which the *Quran* is written. It is thus comprehensible to all Arab-speaking people who have been educated in this language.
30 On 27 Jan 1999, several Algerian cities lost power simultaneously, reportedly to keep residents from watching an *Al Jazeera* programme in which Algerian dissidents implicated the Algerian military in a series of massacres (noted in Wikipedia 'Al Jazeera', Jan 2016).
31 Wikipedia 'Ahmed Ouyahia' website, March 2014.

This situation changed when it came under the control of the Emir of Qatar in 2012.

Although Algerian newspapers are aggressive in their coverage of local affairs, the government uses various methods to punish those critical of the regime. It enforces strict anti-defamation laws and influences content through the state-owned printing press and advertising company. Many of the newspapers are owned by generals.

EUROPEAN REACTIONS

France has had an uneasy relationship with Algeria and has become deeply enmeshed in Algerian affairs, as has become more and more clear over the years. Much is rooted in the history of Algeria and more particularly the War of Independence, and the result has not only been an unsavoury relationship between Algerian individuals, most notably some generals and French politicians and others, but has extended to the corrupt import business called *trabendo*. For Roberts,[32] this is the story of the decline of France's original ambition to establish an exemplary relationship with Algeria to one of conniving at the repression of democratic rights. How has France been able to sustain her pretensions to being the country of human rights? he asks. When I was in France in 2001, relatives of three Algerian disappeared people brought a suit against Nezzar for torture and other crimes: the French organised that he be flown back to Algeria at midnight. Not only has France become deeply enmeshed, and in the most questionable manner, in Algerian affairs, but countries such as the UK took the view that France 'knew all about Algeria', and it seems it was not until late on that the UK may have started to develop its own views. I was told that there was tacit agreement within the EU that France should lead on Maghrebi issues, and especially on Algeria.[33]

32   2003, p 307f.
33   Personal communication in the FCO.

France, together with the West in general, has in the name of
democracy and pluralism, relentlessly undermined the forces of
modern nationalism in Algeria and other countries, endorsing
the most savage repression in the name of modernity and even
of civilisation.[34]

What about the European Union, to which many Algerians
and human rights workers – myself included – turned in hope?
Europe saw economic reform as the cure for Algeria's problems:
its real policy in the early 1990s had been to force the Algerian
government to accept a structural adjustment programme
dictated by the IMF. Even in the late '90s, there were still those
who continued to regard economic reforms as the answer
to Algeria's dire situation. The European Union appeared
ambivalent and unable to produce any coherent view concerning
the state into which Algeria had fallen: resolutions would be
put forward at the European Parliament condemning human
rights abuses in the country, but delegations sent to Algeria, for
example, in early 1998, following the massacres in Bentalha and
Räis, seemed unable to produce any meaningful statement about
what they had found or what they concluded. The President of
the European Parliamentary delegation in February 1998, which
was not of course allowed to visit the site of a massacre, said
that 'we can examine, together with our Algerian colleagues,
the progress made concerning disappearances and arbitrary
arrests.'[35] It was pitiful: they even appeared to sympathise with
the Algerian authorities about an embargo on 'anti-terrorist'
weapons and 'had been convinced that a democracy was
emerging in Algeria.'[36] In public, in Brussels, the EU had always
promoted its concern to uphold political stability, democracy
and respect for human rights – as well as economic reform – in
the southern Mediterranean, launching these as the objectives
of the Euro-Mediterranean Partnership in 1995; this was

---

34   Roberts, 2007, p 314; Roberts mentions Iraq in particular. In his 2003 book, p
     227ff, he provides a lengthy critique of views emanating from the West.
35   *Le Monde,* 19 Feb 1998; ANH 1/98.
36   Roberts, 2003, p 334.

eventually ratified ten or so years later. It was relaunched as the Union for the Mediterranean in 2008, but I had stopped taking an interest in it long before this.

When it had come to some positive solution, or even a serious statement, in the 1990s and later about the human rights situation in Algeria, Europe appeared incapable. It was only some individual MEPs in the European Parliament who put forward highly critical resolutions. It was most instructive – the Algerians were furious and were not about to take any criticism whatsoever. It illustrated how much more might have been done in the European Parliament (and perhaps in our own and others in Europe).

It is now clear that the UK had favoured its own economic interests and acquiesced in the Algerian regime's 'Dirty War' of the 1990s.[37] BP had signed a 'joint venture' with Sonatrach in 1995, in the midst of some of the worst violence after the 1992 putsch... this signature has framed both the British government's and BP's engagement with Algeria over the past twenty years. BP's eagerness to break into Algeria in the 1990s, despite the violent crackdown being enacted by the state, indicated the priorities of the British establishment.

---

37   9 Feb 2014: Arts Activism Education Research: Reinforcing dictatorships – Britain's Gas Grab and Human Rights Abuses in Algeria. In the late 1990s, I had been asked by Sir Geoffrey Chandler, whom I had known in Trinidad and who had formed a 'Business Group' within AIUK with the aim of working with multi-national companies to improve their performance in human rights, to join his group. I had several meetings with the BP London manager for Algerian operations and it was clear that he had little understanding of how BP's operations there impinged on the human rights situation.

7

A CIVILIAN PRESIDENT AND
'A CHARTER FOR PEACE' (1999-2019)

President Zeroual had unexpectedly announced in September 1998 that he would resign and that there would be an election. There was a hiatus of several months and it became clear that there was infighting among *le pouvoir* while they chose their selected President-elect.[1]

All candidates for the 1999 presidential elections, except Abdelaziz Bouteflika, withdrew, citing fraud concerns. There was in fact no election as such,[2] since the dice were loaded against the other six candidates because the army had decided to select Bouteflika, the 'independent' candidate.[3] He was elected

---

1   Ex-General Khaled Nezzar wrote a book (Abed Charif in the *Quot d'Oran* 20 oct 2003) explaining how Algerian presidents had come to power since 1995 and that presidential elections had been nothing but travesties.

2   All presidential elections, at least since 1992, were 'arranged'.

3   In 1981, Bouteflika had been sued for having stolen Algerian embassies' money between 1965 and 1979; on 8 August 1983, he was found guilty of having taken 60 million dinars during his diplomatic career. His claim that he had done this to build a new foreign affairs building was judged 'fallacious'; he reimbursed some 12 million dinars out of 70 million deposited in a Swiss bank. He was amnestied by President Chadli, given a villa, and all his debt was erased (*El Moudjahid*, 9 Aug 1983).

in April 1999 and the populace had to wait several months more while he chose a government. His difficulties demonstrated only too well the chronic weakness of the Presidency of the Republic:[4] his choice had to be approved by *le pouvoir* and he was also obliged to include some whom he would not have chosen. Belkaïd writes that the 'deciders' chose Bouteflika to be President in 1999 since he was a man like them, as incompetent to rule the country as they themselves.[5] He has been described as unstable, very vindictive with a changeable character, and with an immense ego and ambition. He was aggressive towards those who were intellectually superior, which may be explained by his never completing his secondary school studies. To his credit, he admitted at that time that 'everything is rotten in Algeria', destroyed by 'thieves' and 'profiteers' and that the economy was in the hands of a dozen people.[6] I am not aware that he ever spoke in the same manner again. More than a year later, he had still not formed a government and is reported to have said, "I want to be a head of state and not a quarter of a head of state… the question of a new government is not important."[7]

The constitution allowed for only two five-year terms, but it was changed to allow Bouteflika to continue as President for longer than this. How and why had this come about and who had supported him? In short, he accomplished the mission that the 'deciders' had given him: to improve the image of the army and Algeria and to try to free the 'deciders' from their fear of being taken to an International Court of Justice.[8] This he did through his Charter for Peace and National Reconciliation. He had also improved the position of his 'clan' through his own family, headed by his younger brother and by rich and influential businessmen.

---

4   Roberts, 2003, p 266.
5   Roberts, 2005, p 23.
6   Baudoin Loos in the Belgian Le Soir, 18 Sept 1999 (ANH 5/99).
7   Le Monde, 15 Oct 1999 (ANH 5/99 p 2).
8   Dominique Lagarde, Abdelaziz et les siens. Express Roularta Éditions, 2011.

MORE KILLINGS IN KABYLIA; GOVERNMENT INCOMPETENCE IN
FLOODS AND EARTHQUAKE (2001-3)

The general unrest in Kabylia following the killing of Lounès
Matoub in 1998 came to a head again in April 2001 when a
young secondary school pupil was killed in a police station
in the area where Matoub had been assassinated: more than
sixty others were killed by gendarmes using live ammunition
in rioting that followed, and 300 were wounded – some said
600 or 1,000; the rioters, some very young, went beyond their
claim for the Berber culture in denouncing corruption, the
authorities ('*pouvoir assassin*') and attacking offices of the two
main Berber political parties.[9] Young people without hope were
ready to die because they lacked the minimum to survive; one
said: "You cannot kill us for we are already dead."[10] Many more
were killed in riots that went on for some eighteen months and
continued sporadically thereafter; many localities were quite
devastated. A Commission of inquiry in 2001 put the blame
on the *gendarmerie* but not on any individuals.[11] Roberts says
that Kabylia's local leaders had tried to restore order and that
marches of civilians – one of as many as 500,000 people – took
place totally peacefully. At the same time, there was plenty of
evidence of deliberate and outrageous provocations by the
security forces, which helped to reignite the riots – the brutal
contempt with which the authorities treat ordinary people has
its own expression in the Algerian language: *al-hogra*.[12]

A storm and torrential rains on 10 November 2001 caused
catastrophic floods, particularly in a *wadi* in a poor part of
Algiers; 764 people were officially reported to have died and
another 125 were missing. Teams from France, Morocco and
Tunisia arrived. President Bouteflika had not even offered his

9   José Garçon in Libération, 30 Apr & 2 May 2001; later El Watan, 30 Jun, wrote of
     200 deaths and 5,000 injured (ANH 2 & 3/01).
10   José Garçon in Liberation, 20/31 Mar 2002.
11   El Watan, 9 Aug 2001.
12   Roberts, 2003, p 289ff & 293.

condolences and when, after forty-eight hours, he tried to visit, he was met by volleys of stones and cries of "*pouvoir assassin.*" He put the responsibility for the disaster on God.[13]

Eighteen months later, an earthquake on the evening of 21 May 2003, some 60 km east of Algiers, and centred on Boumerdès, of a magnitude on the Richter scale of 6.8, caused more than 2,200 deaths, injured more than 10,000 and left some 150,000 people homeless.[14] The remarkable relief effort from ordinary Algerians and the international community, which started minutes after the quake, made up for the conspicuous absence of the Algerian authorities – apart from the army – during the first few days. President Bouteflika again ran into stone-throwing and promised that all those affected would be rehoused by winter.[15] After the quake, people died in the tents provided, while six months later the debris had still not been cleared. Six years later, 2,000 people whose homes had been completely demolished were still living in temporary accommodation.[16] Some people had been living in what were called chalets or ghettos in 2009 – how they lived was a state scandal – and twelve years later, 154 families had still not been relocated.[17]

ENDEMIC CORRUPTION: A COMMERCIAL EMPIRE COLLAPSES (2002...)

Abdelmoumen Rafik Khalifa, son of an ex-Algerian minister, had built – apparently from nothing – an empire in aeronautics, banks, pharmaceuticals, car-hire and the media.[18] The empire

---

13   El Watan, 19 Nov 2001.
14   AFP, 22-24 May 2003, Le Monde, 24 May 2003 and others (ANH 03/03) on which this section is based.
15   El Watan, 21 May 2013 (ten years later): the effects of the Boumerdes earthquake were still only too visible.
16   El Watan, 21 May 2009.
17   El Watan, 21 May 2015.
18   Jacques Follorou, Le Monde, 24 Dec 2013.

was built up with massive advertising, making use of television and cinema stars, and demonstrated the financial success of Algeria in the world. Officially, the Khalifa group had a turnover of a billion dollars and a profitability of 20%. But a French anti-laundering inquiry found that Khalifa Airways had 'fed' the rest of the group since May 1999. Everything fell apart in 2002, starting with the Khalifa Bank, into which ordinary Algerians had placed so many savings because of the interest it promised to pay. Three collaborators were arrested when trying to leave Algiers Airport with 2 million euros in cash in their bags. The Khalifa group was nothing but a 'Ponzi' scheme, financed by industrialists, small savers and others attracted by the high rate of interest. Some 20,000 staff in Algeria and Europe lost their jobs without recompense but by this time Rafik Khalifa had moved to London. There was a trial in Algeria in 2007, at which Khalifa, *in absentia*, was charged with corruption and sentenced to life imprisonment. He was also wanted by the French authorities.

Khalifa had not awaited the collapse of his empire to install himself comfortably in London, where he lived a luxurious life – he had taken €50 million from his bank and was protected by Her Majesty from extradition by claiming political asylum.[19] After twelve years in London, Khalifa was extradited to Algeria on 24 December 2013, where he awaited trial.

Khalifa was condemned to eighteen years' imprisonment in 2015.[20] The lawyer Me Khaled Bourayou found that few expected this[21] and said that it was a reasonable result. Benyoucef Mellouk,[22] previously a director at the Ministry of Justice, said that the verdict would only be credible when all the senior persons of the country who were implicated in the affair were called to the witness box just like ordinary citizens.

---

19   El Watan, 18 Dec 13, states that Khalifa knew the complexities of the British legal system.
20   Me Khaled Bourayou: 'La peine de Khalifa confirme la thèse du deal.'
21   http://www.algeria-watch.org/fr/article/eco/khalifa/deal.htm
22   El Watan, 23 Jun 2015.

A 'CHARTER FOR PEACE'

President Zeroual had worked hard to try to obtain peace, and the leader of one of the two major armed groups at the time, the AIS, publically supported by the *FIS*, had ordered combat operations to cease in 1997. But neither the other major armed group at the time, the *GIA*, nor clans in the army, were willing to follow suit, and Zeroual resigned as we have seen. Abdelaziz Bouteflika was able to take advantage of this when he became president and amnestied combatants through a disputed '*concorde civile*' or Civil Reconciliation Law in 1999. About 5,500 members of armed groups surrendered in the second half of 1999; some 4,500 of these had been members of the *GIA* and other armed groups.[23]

La sale guerre was presented as a 'national tragedy' with nobody responsible or culpable – as though up to 200,000 deaths and perhaps 18,000 disappearances were of little importance. Nobody has ever been charged or judged for these crimes. In 2006, Bouteflika put before the Algerian public his '**Charter for Peace and National Reconciliation**'. The plan gave hope to millions of Algerians, but it undermined the chance for reconciliation. In speaking of the Charter to *El Watan*,[24] Me Ali-Yahia Abdennour, who is regarded by *El Watan* as '*Monsieur Droits de l'Homme*' (Mr Human Rights) in Algeria, said in strong terms that "it should have been a grand political project (but) was reduced to its purely security dimension." The imperatives of truth and justice were sacrificed and the Charter gave impunity to the military, the *gendarmes* and the police.[25] But the vast majority of the population voted for the Charter because they hoped for peace, and indeed, looking back, the violence gradually diminished, from 2,700 deaths in 2,000 to 670 in 2004. However, in late 2006, the *GSPC* announced its allegiance to *al-Qaida* and in January

23   Amnesty International, 2009, p 12.
24   El Watan, 22 Aug 2007, 'La maladie du Président doit être abordée'.
25   Precisely those who were responsible for the disappearances.

2007 said that it would henceforth be known as *al-Qaida au pays du Maghreb islamique* (*AQMI*). Attacks increased again: there were thirty-eight deaths and more than 200 wounded in the *Palais du gouvernement,* and sixty-eight deaths at the UNO office in Algiers.

For Bouteflika, the Charter was a success: he had pleased the 'deciders' and there would not be an inquiry into the recent actions of the military – nor into the violence of radical Islamists. It also pleased the majority of the Algerian population since it gradually brought about peace for most. But the Decree effectively denied victims, including families of the disappeared, the right to any remedy for serious human rights violations, in contravention of Article 8 of the Universal Declaration of Human Rights. It remained dangerous as late as 2018 to denounce police violence. Rafik Belamrania was condemned to five years in prison in February 2017 for publishing, on Facebook, the results of the UN Human Rights Committee condemning the Algerian State for the summary execution of his father in 1995.[26] In complete contrast, some 2,200 people who had been charged with or convicted of involvement in terrorist activities were freed from detention in March 2006.

It was at this time in the early 2000s that a polemic was going on in the British parliament and elsewhere over the Blair government's proposal to extradite imprisoned Algerians back to Algeria, many of whom had never been charged with an offence: they had been held on the basis of secret information. In December 2004, the Lords had judged their detention illegal; they were freed and detained again on the basis that they constituted a menace to British security.[27]

---

26 He was freed a year later. François Gèze et Salima Mellah, Algeria-Watch, 22 Feb 2019.

27 Many were held following the bombing of underground trains and a bus in London on 7 July 2005.

LIFE IN ALGERIA FOR ORDINARY PEOPLE, AND THE
DETERMINATION TO EMIGRATE (HARRAGA)

Abderrahmane X (a pseudonym), an Algerian exiled in France, visited Algiers and reported on life there as he found it in 2006. He wrote that millions living in *bidonvilles* were desperate for bread, a roof or water in order to survive, and every way of making money was good. But many of the 'middle class' were in a similar situation, and for the majority of salaried people their monthly pay lasted only a week: the rest of the time they were reduced to working in the black market or by borrowing. Money or the lack of it was the principal source of conflicts, murders, divorces. Insecurity reigned. The people lived in such misery that it was acceptable to do anything for money, to be in the black market and to sell drugs, arms and medicaments. The population had been abandoned by the state and could only count upon itself for what was necessary.[28] What one noticed in Algiers was that the state was absent. Women who had been beaten, humiliated or thrown in the streets were more and more numerous, for there was nowhere they could go for help. Nobody knew what the consequences would be on the children in ten or twenty years.

El Watan reported that ninety-eight *bidonvilles* had arisen in the Tizi Ouzou region of Kabylia.[29] They were populated by hundreds of families, many of whom were without sanitation, drinking water, electricity or other services, insupportably cold in winter and infernally hot in summer, open to all sorts of illnesses; children were especially liable to such illnesses. Some families had been there for forty years.

In 2011, it was reported that one third of young people

---

28 Ten years later, in 2016, Salima Mellah wrote that hundreds of thousands of people had been rehoused in newly built apartments, but many found they had arrived in 'hell'– in suburbs where they were not welcome, are far from the city – and isolation and ostracism nourish violence among the young. http://www.algeria-watch.org/fr/article/analyse/mellah_crise_logement.htm

29 3 Jan 2008.

dreamt of going to Europe: most of these were well educated and didn't come from the poorer classes. To unemployment was added an almost total lack of places to meet: there were only two cinemas in Algiers at the time and the city closed at 2000 hrs – except for cybercafes, which become fewer and fewer. So the young had to watch television at home where there were typically seven to eight persons living in only two rooms.[30] The marriage age was already thirty-two for men and twenty-eight for women in 2010, in a society that had married in the very early twenties (younger, for women). A woman cannot marry without the agreement of a guardian, and polygamy is still allowed. Girls are now more likely to go to university than boys.

Civil Society *associations* estimated the number of Algerians living below the poverty line in 2016 to be 10 million. Nobody can claim to know the real number, but M Houari, National Secretary of the *LADDH*, is 'persuaded' that the number was one Algerian in three in 2015.[31] Another study, carried out by the University of Algiers in December 2014, indicated the number to be one in two Algerians (20 million).

Large numbers of young unemployed Algerians, without hope for the future, attempt to cross the Mediterranean. They are called **harraga** (or *harga,* from the Arabic, meaning to 'destroy their papers') and many try and cross in most unsuitable boats and are drowned. It was probably in 2007-8 that it became noticeable just how many were trying to cross the Mediterranean. Michael Busch wrote[32] that 'in 2007 alone, over 50,000 young Algerians reportedly attempted to flee their homeland... over 90 percent of them will either die at sea, be arrested and detained indefinitely in Tunisia or Libya, or be returned by the Algerian,

---

30 Lagarde, 2011, p 33ff. The number of rooms quoted in a flat or house in France (and presumably also in Algeria) does not include the kitchen or bathroom but it does, of course, include the sitting room.

31 http://www.algeria-watch.org/pdf/pdf_fr/laddh_seuil_pauvrete.pdf

32 Foreign Policy in Focus, 25 Jan 2011, from WikiLeaks cable XXXIII. http://fpif.org/wikileaks_xxxiii_algerias_youth_too_dazed_and_confused_to_even_become_terrorists/ The article gives more information gleaned by embassy staff (presumably American) collecting first-hand information of the human trafficking network that transports hundreds of Algerians to Europe each month.

French, Spanish or Italian coastguards.'

El Watan[33] wrote that the Algerian NGO *LADDH* had announced that there were some 600 bodies in Spanish morgues in Alicante, Almeria and other places further south in Spain.[34] "If Algeria had done nothing for them while they were alive, at least they could repatriate them to their own country," said the President of the Commission for the Safeguard of Algerian Youth. BBC Radio 4[35] interviews in the Annaba area (on the Mediterranean coast close to Tunisia) and in Algiers reported that local people tried to migrate to Sardinia because "we have no life in Algeria," "we can't find jobs," "there is no hope." "In Europe, there is respect for others, they have human rights; life is a prison here." The programme told us that the price to go in a small boat to Sardinia would be of the order of $1,000, which could be less if there were more people wanting to go there. An article in May 2018 suggested that the number wishing to leave is continuously increasing.[36]

To the south of the country, large numbers of migrants have been leaving West Africa and crossing the Sahara to Algeria seeking a better life. *El Watan*[37] says that they are fleeing failed countries with poor government, corruption, climate change and other failings and are met with hostility: African countries, of which Algeria is one, cause this situation. It must become a welcoming country. AI wrote that the Algerian authorities had forcibly expelled more than 2,000 sub-Saharan migrants, including 300 minors, from a range of countries, to Mali and Niger in the first weeks of October 2017.[38]

---

33 http://www.algeria-watch.org/fr/article/pol/migration/600_harraga_morgues.htm and many other sites on Algeria-Watch.

34 The LADDH said that they were doing what they could to repatriate the bodies before the Spanish incinerated them.

35 BBC Radio 4 in Crossing Continents broadcast: The Harragas of Algeria, 24 Aug 2015.

36 Pourquoi partent-ils ? El Watan, 29 May 2018

37 12 Jul 2017, http://www.algeria-watch.org/fr/article/pol/migration/devoir_solidarite.htm.

38 www.amnesty.org/en/latest/news/2017/10/algeria

SONATRACH: CORRUPTION AT THE HIGHEST LEVEL AND THE
SIXTY-YEAR OIL AND GAS BONANZA ENDS[39]

New fields discovered in the 1990s[40] and then, from the year 2000 by BP and its partners far to the south at In Salah, gave rise to significant new oil and gas exports for the country. In 2014, Algeria was the tenth largest oil producer in the world and in 2013, the tenth largest producer of natural gas, but between 2005 and 2014, Sonatrach lost a huge portion of its gas market. Hocine Malti,[41] who had been Vice President of Hydrocarbons of Sonatrach, said in 2010 that for a good fifteen years, the quantities of new oil discovered could not replace what had already been produced.

Malti wrote[42] that the appointment of 'Tewfik' in September 1990 to head the Secret Services meant that the 'DAF' clan came to control Algeria's oil and gas business totally. 'Tewfik' owed his career to Larbi Belkheir and did what Belkheir wanted. One of the main tasks 'Tewfik' was given was to place Sonatrach under the direct control of the DRS – it should have been the responsibility of the Minister of Energy. The two friends succeeded in casting a veil over what was going on in the petroleum business and its billions of dollars' revenue; this allowed them to conceal all sorts of malpractices and to divert an important part to their personal profit and that of their clan. They could build up a 'black box' to finance doubtful operations: corruption, allocating sums of money to the chiefs of armed groups so that they could change sides. They could lay their hands on millions of dollars, especially from foreign companies wanting to obtain acreage in the most promising areas. Belkheir was able to have a trusted man appointed Head of Sonatrach; no Prime Minister nor any Ministry of Energy during the period 1989-95 could impose any decision which didn't please Belkheir and 'Tewfik'.

39   See Malti's *Histoire secrète du pétrole algérien* for a review of oil and gas in Algeria since its discovery in the 1950s.
40   These may well have resulted from the Robertson Research report designed for this purpose.
41   Malti, 2010, p 301f. Malti left the position of Vice President of Hydrocarbons in Sonatrach and moved to a senior position in Kuwait and later to Libya.
42   2010, p 301ff.

Many foreign companies arrived to explore for oil and gas from 1990, the most notable being Anardarko, a small Texan company, which – in four years – made the most important discovery since Hassi Messaoud in 1956.[43] These foreign companies all had to pay commissions, often very substantial, to godfathers – one of the generals.[44] The 'deciders' could only rejoice at the discoveries, which increased sales and augmented their 'commissions'. It was at this time that Algerian oil ceased to be the property of the Algerian people, to become the property of a *mafioso* group.

The government had, at least since 2008, decided to exploit what is called schist or shale gas, but as so often happens in Algeria, this only became public knowledge much later. It was on 31 December 2014 that the Algerian people in the Sahara took to the streets of the main towns of In Salah and Ouargla (and elsewhere) and protested about the government's decisions to begin fracking for oil and gas, which had taken place in complete secrecy.[45] Protests were still going on months later. Sonatrach and the government congratulated themselves on the result of the first test drilling, but the manner in which the operator left the site (handling of toxic chemicals and other materials) was disgraceful.[46] However, the major question for local people was that of groundwater: ancestral users of the desert had developed systems of irrigation that allowed desert dwellers to use groundwater safely, and a local spokesman said that "the exploitation of shale gas will destroy this treasure." When peaceful protestors went to the Halliburton base to deliver a letter on 28 February 2015, *gendarmes* insulted them racially and chased them away: stones were thrown against teargas and the violence moved to the town. The handling of the environment became a national, and not just a Saharan, concern.

---

43   The find was some 100 km southeast of Hassi Messaoud. Anadarko had two minority partners: Lasmo (British) and Maersk (Danish). Various other very significant discoveries meant that Anadarko became the second most important company in Algeria after Sonatrach (Malti, p 303).

44   Malti, 2010, p 289.

45   Salima Mellah, 16 Apr 2015, Quand l'avenir de l'Algérie s'oppose au gaz de schiste.

46   Almost nothing corrodes or dissolves on the surface of the desert, and everything must be treated with the greatest care and respect and carefully removed (my own experience working in that environment in Libya).

Algeria's finances and the state of the economy are entirely dependent on the oil and gas discovered and produced, and the price that it receives for these resources. There were massive increases in price in the 1970s due to the action of OPEC, and prices thereafter increased and fell as world demand increased or decreased. From 2011, the price remained in the US$90 – $120 range for three years until mid-2014, when prices declined precipitously, firstly due to increased production (and fracking in the USA), and secondly due to declining demand in 'emerging' countries. By February 2016, the oil price was below US$30 – a drop of almost 75% since mid 2014 – as competing producers, including Algeria, continued exporting, while OPEC, led by Saudi Arabia, did not react to the reduced demand. The effect upon Algeria's economy and balance of payments was stark. The Vice President of the IMF considered that 'the Algerian economy faced a serious shock that potentially could last several years, require reductions in expenditure and vast reforms.'[47]

The first scandal within the oil and gas business had begun during Boumediène's presidency and related to the construction of a major liquefaction plant (Arzew); this involved a friend of Boumediène's, an American firm and a commission of $2.75mn on a $300mn contract, but it was not until 2007/8 that details became open knowledge.[48] Malti[49] tried to explain how, 'behind the pompous words of the struggle against corruption, exorbitant bribes have been filling bank accounts of senior government officials' pockets.'[50]

---

47   Yacine Babouche, TSA, 21 Jan 2016: Les grands médias internationaux s'interrogent sur l'avenir de l'Algérie.

48   Malti, 2010, p 224f.

49   Malti, 2010, p 10.

50   Patrick Cockburn: 'Ridding the world of corruption cannot be done until we tackle the resource rich' (the Independent 14 May 2016) seems to be most relevant to Algeria. Cockburn begins by asking if corruption can be controlled by reform – he is referring to the anti-corruption summit which took place in London in May 2016. He ends the article by concluding that where there is no accountability or a fair legal system, corruption cannot be tamed since it is at the heart of the system. Cockburn's article is largely based on a book by Tom Burgis (The Looting Machine: Warlords, Tycoons, Smugglers and the Systematic Theft of Africa's Wealth), who writes that the politically powerful live parasitically off state revenues and are not accountable to anyone: the outcome of a government acquiring great wealth without doing more than license foreign companies to pump oil or excavate minerals is devastating.

Sonatrach became hit by increasing scandals and in January 2010 its Chief Executive was put under judicial review, and almost all of its senior management was removed, some jailed. In August of the same year, Chekib Khelil, the Algerian Energy Minister, his wife and two sons were charged and international warrants issued for their arrest.[51] The charges related to corruption, money laundering, irregularities in the award of contracts, abuse of office and the creation of organised criminal gangs. Charges were also brought against the Italian firm SAIPEM and the Egyptian firm Orascom Industries; the judicial investigation has established that there was a global network that took bribes in exchange for contracts with Sonatrach – colossal sums were allegedly charged by intermediaries who were officials at the Energy Ministry or Sonatrach.[52] The arrest warrant for Khelil was annulled in December 2013[53] but *Le Soir d'Algerie*[54] announced that an international arrest warrant had been launched in Milan and

---

51 Malti 2010 p 308ff. Chekib Khelil was born in Morocco of Algerian parents and spent much of his early years with his friend Abdelaziz Bouteflika in Morocco. Having grown up together, the two remained close. Abdelaziz helped Khelil obtain a grant to study in the USA, where he obtained a PhD in petroleum engineering and a job with a respected reservoir engineering company. Approached by Sonatrach, he joined the national company in 1973, where he obtained senior jobs under Hocine Malti. It was the first time in his life that he had been in Algeria. When Chadli became president, Khelil returned to the USA to work for the World Bank (WB). His recommendation to the Argentinian government that they should sell the national oil company YPFB was disastrous for that country. After twenty years at the WB, he was offered the position of Algerian Energy and Mines Minister by Bouteflika, who then made him his Advisor. It was at this time that Bouteflika established close relations with the USA. Malti writes that Khelil was a good petroleum engineer but a poor manager and a mediocre politician; he is more feared than respected in the Energy sector. He lacks tact, bears grudges and has made many enemies. With all his connections with the USA, Khelil is considered by Algerian public opinion (and many senior Algerians) as an American 5th column in the power structure.

52 Algeria: former Minister charged in Sonatrach corruption case: Magharebia (Washington DC), 16 Aug 2013.

53 Algeria-Watch. L'affaire Chekib Khelil: quand la justice est au service du régime. Boubekeur Ait Benali, 3 Dec 2013. http://www.algeria-watch.org/fr/article/eco/corruption/khelil_justice_au_service.htm

54 Algeria-Watch. Le parquet de Milan lance la procédure, 16 Feb 2014.

that the American Securities and Exchange were also about to charge Khelil.[55]

Khelil returned freely to Algeria on 17 March 2016[56] and started on a tour of the whole country. An article in *El Watan* (a newspaper supported by the military) argues that this must have been organised by the presidential clan and the international arrest warrants annulled. Saïd Bouteflika, brother of the President, through *Ennehar* TV, announced that Khelil would be rehabilitated to take an important post after having been *sali* (lit: 'dirtied') by the *DRS*: he had decided to return because all the officers who had plotted against him had been 'dismissed'.

Hocine Malti[57] wrote that the scenario that Khelil had been sent to Algeria to take up the position of Prime Minister, or even of President, by the USA, seemed to be being put in place.[58] It is, perhaps, part of a plan concocted in concert between Algiers and Washington: 'there is a fire in the house' (referring to Bouteflika being totally incapacitated); we must act quickly without quibbling too much about legal matters. Khelil had lived in Algeria only some seventeen years of his life and so long in the USA that he had come to be known as 'the American'.

Khelil's return coincided closely with the publication of what were called the **'Panama Papers'**: these named twenty-two Algerians who had offshore companies domiciled in Panama. These included Chekib Khelil's wife, Mme Najat Arafat, his

---

55 Algeria-Watch, 26 Jan 2016 has more information about this case, which had been going on for three years at the time of writing: Affaire Saipem : Le parquet milanais déboute Sonatrach. http://www.algeria-watch.org/fr/article/eco/corruption/parquet_milanais.htm – The affair is about commissions of €198m paid for gas contracts to the value of €8 billion; it concerns executives of SAIPEM, a subsidiary of the Italian national company ENI and three Algerians: ex-Energy Minister Chakib Khelil, Farid Bediaoui – who negotiated with SAIPEM – and Samir Ourayed. The Milan public prosecutor's office is leading investigations into a 'vast corruption network' implicating numerous top Italian petroleum executives and the entourage of Chakib Khelil.

56 Retour au pays en toute impunité, El Watan, 18 Mar 2016. http://www.algeria-watch.org/fr/article/eco/corruption/khelil_retour_pays.htm

57 Le cadeau empoisonné des Etats-Unis à l'Algérie, 6 May 2016 http://www.algeria-watch.org/fr/article/analyse/malti_cadeau_empoisonne.htm

58 Malti http://www.algeria-watch.org/fr/article/analyse/malti_cadeau_empoisonne.htm

nephew Réda Hemche and two close associates of Khelil: Farid Bejaoui and Omar Habour. Moncef Wafi[59] wrote that Khelil's wife passed two offshore companies she owned to Omar Habour and made moves in Panama so that bank accounts in Switzerland would be kept secret. The sum of $198m is mentioned as being passed to companies in Hong Kong created for Farid Bedjaoui (by Mossack Fonseca, the financier at the centre of the scandal); the name of Bedjaoui appears in at least seventeen offshore companies, domiciled in Panama, the British Virgin Isles and the UAE. The Algerian Association against Corruption (AACC)[60] states that Khelil, according to the 'Panama Papers' is implicated in contracts of billions of euros in Italy and Spain, in which commissions of 3% could be obtained.[61] More exposure of fortunes being hidden in Spain, the Virgin Isles and elsewhere came to light in 2017.[62]

THE 'ARAB SPRING' (2011) AND AN INCAPABLE PRESIDENT RE-ELECTED (2014)[63]

On 18 December 2010, Mohamed Bouazizi, a street vendor in Tunisia, set himself alight in protest at how his wares were being confiscated and how he was being treated by the local authorities.

---

59 Le Quotidien d'Oran: Paradis fiscal au Panama: 22 Algériens cités dans le scandale des <Panama papers>, 11 May 2016.

    A later article published by Le Soir d'Algérie (What Algerians think of the corruption affairs, 29 May 2016') http://www.algeria-watch.org/aw-info/phplist/lt.php?id=Nx0EAgtZS1cICxlSVQ5e) states that the Panama Papers include '200 other unknown Algerians'. Lakhdar Bouagaâ, a hero of the Algerian Revolution said, "We have a veritable mafia which is organised and specialist in all sectors and which is specialist in corruption." Among others mentioned in the Panama Papers list are Abdeslam Bouchouareb, the son of ex-President Chadli, the daughter of the Prime Minister Abdelmalek Sellal and Ammar Saâdani Secretary General of the FLN.

60 http://www.algeria-watch.org/aw-info/phplist/lt.php?id=Nx0EAghQS1cIBRlSVQ5e

61 The Spanish contracts were said by the AACC and others to implicate the King of Spain and a German 'Princess'.

62 http://www.algeria-watch.org/fr/article/eco/corruption/fortunes_cachees_exterieur.htm El Watan, 27 Jul 2017.

63 Algérie : la fin de règne pitoyable et dangereuse d'un régime décadent. Hocine Malti, Algeria-Watch, 10 Jan 2015

This act came to be regarded as the start of what was called the 'Arab Spring', with protests and riots spreading : a regime change in Tunisia, a government change in Egypt, the killing of Gaddafi and a near civil war in Libya, and perhaps worse in Syria. It was noted in the West that there was no comparable 'Arab Spring' in Algeria and the country was regarded by many as a country of stability. This was hardly how Algerians saw it: there had been continuous unrest,[64] there had been five days of rioting in January 2011 and widespread riots throughout the country following an increase in price of basic necessities. The government's response was to restore food subsidies and increase state salaries.

Algerians had impatiently awaited a speech by President Bouteflika on 15 April 2011 since this would be the first time he had spoken following the 'Arab Spring'. He announced that there would be a revision of laws concerning political parties, of the electoral *code* and – most importantly – of the Constitution, in order "to reinforce democracy." Reporters seem to have been more interested in the President's poor health than in what he had say.[65]

As has been noted, violence had continued during the fifteen years of Bouteflika's first three terms as President, lessening or increasing but rarely making headlines in the international press. A state of emergency that had lasted nearly twenty years ended.[66] Despite being frequently hospitalised in Paris[67] and having hardly spoken in public since 2012, Bouteflika subsequently became president for a fourth term in 2014. He was elected on 9 April 2014, officially winning, it was announced, 85% of the vote. The *DRS* remained the central institution supervising all others, civilian and military, including the presidency of the

---

64 *Algérie 2012 : un régime de vieillards sanguinaires en fin de règne* http://www.algeria-watch.org/fr/aw/fin_de_regne.htm

65 Le Monde, 15 Apr 2011, and Courrier international, 18 Apr 2011.

66 Did the ending of the State of Emergency, which had done so much to weaken civil society and had allowed so many violations of human rights to take place, bring any more freedom to Algerian life? The answer must be 'no'. Harrassment by police, the prevention of public meetings and abusive administrative practices continued. The ending of the State of Emergency should have been a positive move for the better but it has not been (Réseau euro-méditerrean des droits de l'Homme).

67 Only Tewfik visited him in hospital. Laribi p 209.

Republic. The President could not even name his own *Chef de cabinet* (Principal Private Secretary).[68] When he has appeared in recent years, very rarely and only briefly on television, he has been pitifully made up to try to give a natural air to occasional hand movements.

There are a variety of views about what is happening during what must surely be an 'end-of-regime' situation. These different views illustrate how little is really known about Bouteflika's fourth presidential term from 2014:

- Lahouari Addi[69]wrote in January 2016 that the President 'doesn't speak, doesn't hear, and doesn't know what day it is; this shows that the system functions without a president and that the Algerian state is run by government officials appointed by the army. The army is the source of power, and has a service which runs society politically, the *DRS*. Bouteflika has no power.' There is no struggle between clans: the battle against Islamist violence in the 1990s gave rise to the power lying with the *DRS*: *DRS* staff have so much power that a colonel of an operational unit is afraid of a *DRS* lieutenant, who is in theory his subordinate. Bouteflika remains in post due to a desire to die there and have a state funeral.
- Malti[70] asks: who is representing the President at international events, who signs legislation for him or who works between the different clans? Perhaps it is the least dangerous and feeblest: the Prime Minister Abdelmalek Sellal.[71]

---

68   *http://www.algeria-watch.org/fr/aw/fin_de_regne.htm*

69   Lahouari Addi, 9 Jan 2016. http://www.algeria-watch.org/fr/article/mil/addi__ retraite_Tewfik.htm

70   Algérie : la fin de règne pitoyable et dangereuse d'un régime décadent. Algeria-Watch, 10 Jan 2015: http://www.algeria-watch.org/fr/aw/malti_fin_de_regne.htm

71   UK Prime Minister Cameron was greeted and accompanied by Abdelmalek Sellal (not President Bouteflika) when he visited Algeria on 30 Jan 2013, about the attack on the gas complex of Tiguentourine.

- Sifaoui[72] believes that a violent dispute arose between the presidential clan and that of the *DRS* in February 2014: Bouteflika wanted to ensure the total impunity of his family and clan. There had been much speculation that his younger brother Said would succeed him.

FRENCH MOUNTAIN GUIDE ASSASSINATED IN KABYLIA (2014)

Six months after Bouteflika's re-election in 2014, a quite unexpected and significant assassination occurred in Kabylia – which had been the centre of so much violence in the 1990s and early 2000s. On 22 September 2014, a hastily produced video showed a French mountain guide, Hervé Gourdel, between two armed and hooded men. An ultimatum from an *AQMI* group[73] was addressed to Paris demanding the ending, within twenty-four hours, of French airstrikes against the Islamic State in Iraq. Two days after this, a new video showed the decapitation of Gourdel. Habib Souaïdia, who had concluded that the *DRS* had been responsible for so many of the abuses of the 1990s, investigated the material and wrote that it was again the *DRS*, and not the Islamic State, who had been responsible for the assassination of Gourdel.[74]

Violence has continued sporadically in the 21st century. There were clashes between security forces and armed opposition groups in various areas of Algeria, and security forces were said to have killed 109 alleged members of armed groups; *AQMI* said it carried out an attack in the northern province of Ain Defla in July that killed fourteen soldiers.[75]

---

72 Sifaoui (2014, p 11) spent four years researching the Algerian secret services.
73 The group said, at the end of the month, that it was now a part of the so-called Islamic State.
74 *De l'assassinat d'Hervé Gourdel à la déstabilisation tunisienne : manipulations et intox des services secrets algériens* 27 Apr 15. https://algeria-watch.org/?p=5492
75 AI Annual Report 2015/2016 Algeria.

8

'TERRORISM' IN THE SAHARA AND THE SAHEL

I now turn from northern Algeria, and back to 2003, to the Sahara, and what is called the Sahel – 'the 'southern shore' of the Sahara, which extends from Mauritania to Mali, Niger and beyond. It is an extraordinary story. It begins within Algeria but moves into the adjacent countries of Mali and Niger and later elsewhere in West Africa. We have seen some most terrible acts for which the Military Security, the *DRS*, were responsible, but is it possible that their murderous influence might even extend outside the country's borders? What is the truth behind this story and its dreadful consequences for the Tuareg[1] and other

---

1   The Tuareg are a people living in a large area of adjacent countries – Mali, Burkina Faso, Niger, Algeria, Libya.

indigenous peoples of the area?[2] The difficulty of interpreting so much of what goes on in Algeria is that proof is almost impossible; one has to arrive at the most likely scenario and, when there are sufficient events of a certain nature, to judge whether there really is any other possibility than that one's 'unlikely conclusion' is most likely to be the truth.

This part of the Sahara had become a tourist paradise since the year 2000 when it had been re-opened to foreigners: it is regarded by many as perhaps the most beautiful and remarkable desert landscape in the world. However, the area possesses priceless prehistoric artifacts (stone axes, arrowheads, stone jewellery and figurines, pottery, etc.) which were being stolen and spirited out of the country by the truckload. Paintings and engravings were even being hacked out of rockfaces. The Tuareg's cultural heritage was being destroyed, and their livelihood, which had seen some hope of improvement with these riches, was going with them.[3] A dossier on these criminal acts was compiled by representatives of the United Nations: this made it plain that the looters were mostly European, and the first big 'stash' found was that of a Munich-based operation run by a German. There were German hands in other thefts. The

2   Gèze and Mellah (22 Sept 2007) write about the period up to 2007. Later books by Jeremy Keenan (*The Dark Sahara, 2009* and *The Dying Sahara* 2013a) are about the Algerian Sahara and the Sahel. Much of what I have written is based on this article and books. Jeremy Keenan had been working in the area for decades and is a recognised authority on the nomadic Tuareg – who know what is going on in their lands.

    However, I should note that Thomas Miles (*Death and Career in the 'Dark' Sahara: the Sad Fate of Jeremy Keenan* http://www.tomathon.com/mphp/2012/01/death-and-career-in-the-dark-sahara-the-sad-fate-of-jeremy-keenan/#sthash.mfwRu0nX.dpuf) writes damningly of Keenan's work. He says that 'Keenan... has one answer for all questions, one bad guy and one bad guy only who is behind all disorder and suffering... People who don't know much about northern Mali would be very poorly served by reading Keenan's increasingly odd writing.' Thomas Miles is an independent scholar who lives in New York. His book, *Sahel. A Short History of Mali, Niger and the Lands in Between* is due to be published by Hurst.

3   Many Tuareg, in order to earn a good living, went to Libya to fight for Col Gaddafi; these fighters have returned to Mali since Gaddafi's death, well armed and well trained. Mali had been saying that the fall of Gaddafi would have a destabilising effect in the region (BBC 17 Oct 2011: http://www.bbc.co.uk/news/world-africa-15334088).

dossier was ready for a court of law, but arrests could only be made by catching the criminals red-handed. This had to be done by the Algerian authorities, and copies of the dossier were sent to the government and various Algerian authorities but they took no action. Why not? This is a further strand in the story of Algeria.[4]

TOURISTS KIDNAPPED IN THE SAHARA (2003)

The *GSPC* came to worldwide attention in early 2003 when thirty-two German-speaking European tourists,[5] travelling in seven different groups, were spectacularly kidnapped in the south of the Algerian Sahara, most of them in the area north of the Tassili-n-Ajjer Mountains (north of Tamanrasset – see map).[6] A first group was released in May and a second, who had been taken on a 3,000 kilometre journey into Mali, in July. The hostages reported that they were well looked after, that the kidnappers were 'always polite and never aggressive, wishing to bring the situation in Algeria to international attention.'[7] One woman died of heatstroke at the end of June. There were a number of very strange elements about this affair: no group claimed responsibility, there was no immediate claim for ransom nor any political demand, Algerian army helicopters flew over the two camps of the hostages at low altitude as early as mid-March and the authorities must therefore have known where the hostages were.[8] As seems true of so many things Algerian, there was a tangled web to try and unravel to get at some sort

---

4   Keenan, 2009, pp 10-12.
5   Fifteen German, ten Austrian, four Swiss, one Swede, one Dutchman and the woman who died from the heat.
6   It was reported in mid-April that the Algerian authorities had launched a massive search involving 7,000 people – 5,000 of them soldiers – to comb the area (ANH, 02/03, p 1 reporting a number of French and Algerian sources).
7   ANH, 03/03, p 1 (*Quotidien d'Oran* 18, 19 May, 24 Jun; *Le Matin* 17, 26 May, 26 Jun).
8   Salima Mellah, *Algérie 2003: L'affaire des 'otages du Sahara', décryptage d'une manipulation.*

of truth of what had happened. It is another story that does no credit to the Algerian authorities. But neither do the American authorities come out of it well.

There was naturally much speculation as to which group was responsible for the kidnapping. The Algerian press stated early on that the only known group in the area was that led by Mokhtar ben Mokhtar, a man known as *MBM*, whose death had been reported by the Algerian authorities on at least six occasions since the mid-1990s, who had had many aliases and nicknames, and was reputedly linked to Hassan Hattab's *GSPC*. *MBM* effectively controlled this part of southern Algeria and the northern Sahel regions of Niger, Mali and Mauritania by having a near-stranglehold over the contraband business in drugs, vehicles and the running of much of the huge trans-Saharan smuggling businesses.[9]

The Algerian authorities put out contradictory and confusing statements – their *forte*. Having said that a band of smugglers was responsible, they did not mention *MBM* but announced on 10 July that the leader of the kidnappers was '*El Para*', a name derived from his time as a parachutist in the Algerian army. They said that the hostages had been released in a gun battle, but it turned out to have been just a theatrical performance.[10] It has been said[11] that *El Para* was a *DRS* agent who might also have been a US Green Beret trained at Fort Bragg in the 1990s and that he was not an Islamist but was working for the Algerian secret military services. After the release of the second group of hostages, for which it is said that a ransom was paid,[12] serious questions arose: why was *El Para* allowed to flee into Niger, Chad and – apparently Libya, but was never picked up

---

9   Keenan, 2009, pp 21-23.
10 This could be confirmed when the state of vehicles used by the German hostages were investigated in Germany.
11 Keenan 2009 p 101.
12 First reports said that the ransom was paid by Libya, Mali or another country, to be repaid by Germany in the form of development aid (ANH 04/03: Hostages liberated).

by the authorities?[13] Why had there never been any demand for payment by the kidnappers – the usual reason for kidnapping?[14] Virtually every statement issued by the Algerians, from the 16th May[15] until confirmation that they were in Mali in a German radio report on 18 July, was false. Why were the second group of hostages – whose release had been announced by the authorities and then denied hours later by the same authorities – taken on the extraordinary journey to Mali?[16] The story outdoes almost any 'whodunnit'.[17]

The GSPC, founded in 1998, had gradually supplanted the GIA.[18] As already noted, the GSPC had at first been active in the north of Algeria where it targeted the security forces only. Later, civilians and foreigners also became targets.[19] It became internationally notorious with the kidnapping of the tourists in the Sahara in 2003, and came to be regarded as a menace to Europe. It was around this time that the GSPC took on the name of AQMI, and it became clear that it was a creation of the Algerian secret services, the DRS, whose chiefs had been the real power in the land since the 1992 putsch. The history of the GSPC from 1998 to 2007 can be explained by the struggle between the clans of le pouvoir for control of the oil and gas riches of Algeria. 'Tewfik', who had been head of the DRS since 1990, had seen his

13   He was eventually tried 'in absentia' in Algeria, a trial that told us nothing and was evidently designed for that purpose – it would have been much too dangerous to allow him to have given any evidence.

14   It was reported that El Para had been paid €4.6mn for the release of the tourists (Algeria-Watch, 20 Dec 2008: Où sont passés Hassan Hattab et Amari Saïfi alias Abderrezak El Para?).

15   Date of the annulled statement of release of the second group.

16   In The Dying Sahara, Keenan (p 160f) states that BOB, who was connected with a burnt-out drug-carrying Boeing 727 in Mali in 2009, 'had been at the centre of every hostage negotiation in Mali since El Para brought his fourteen European hostages into the region in 2003.'

17   The local peoples of this part of the Sahara – the Tuareg, well known to Keenan, who had been studying there for decades – did not recognise the picture that the Algerian intelligence-media painted of their region over the period; they know that most, if not all, of the alleged 'terrorist' incidents had been exaggerated or fabricated.

18   Gèze, François et Mellah, Salima, 22 Sept 2007.

19   In retrospect, it now seems likely that this was when the GSPC came under the control of the DRS.

pre-eminence contested by the Bouteflika clan, who challenged the privileged position that 'Tewfik' tied up with the USA. Hence the 'Tewfik' clan's choice to destabilise the Bouteflika clan and to increase the 'terrorist' actions of *GSPC-AQMI*, including against foreign targets. Lahouari Addi, among others, denies that there was any struggle between clans; there was, he writes, a rearrangement of the organisation of the army. But he does say that within the struggle against violence, the *DRS* came to have a greater political weight over the army. However that may be, it seems quite clear that the seizure of the tourists was yet another act of state terrorism.

THE UNITED STATES AND STATE TERRORISM IN WEST AFRICA

The media so often asks the questions: 'Who was responsible and what was happening?' but the more important question, not always asked, is: Why? Why had the Sahel, previously largely peaceful, become an area, according to George W Bush, infested with terrorists? And why was the *DRS* apparently colluding with the USA there? We need to go back to 1998, when the reliance of the USA on foreign oil imports surpassed the psychologically critical level of 50%: this was the first time that more than half of the country's oil was imported from overseas and was a matter of national concern.[20] The expectation was that the reliance of the country on foreign imports would increase over time and, as a result, George W Bush made it an election issue in the year 2000 and, following this, pledged to make energy security a top priority of his presidency. Within two weeks of taking office, he established a National Energy Policy Development Group, under the chairmanship of Vice-President Dick Cheney,[21] which

---

20 Since then the discovery of fracking in the USA has increased production enormously and the country has hardly needed outside oil.

21 Vice President 2001-9; he had been Secretary of Defense under George H W Bush 1989-Jan 93 and, as an important part of this story, had been CEO of Halliburton 1995-2000, one of the world's largest oil services companies and active in Algeria and the Sahel.

identified West Africa as a major new source of oil imports. Bush's administration defined African oil as a strategic national interest and thus a resource that the US might choose military force to control. It was just at this time that the coordinated attack by the Islamic *al-Qaida* group on the United States took place on 11 September 2001 ('9/11') and the world's attention became focussed on this, to the exclusion of just about all else.

It was following the 9/11 attack and the UN placing the *GSPC* on the UN list of terrorist organisations in 2002, that it is claimed the *DRS* chiefs thought of exporting their 'residual terrorism' into the Sahara.[22] The kidnapping of thirty-two European tourists was 'a spectacular success' for the *DRS* since it took Maghreb terrorism to the Sahel via the Sahara and to a 'new Afghanistan' where *al-Qaida* was apparently already established. This allowed Algeria to become an ally of the Bush administration, to obtain the latest military equipment and to become a major player in the 'Global War against Terrorism' (GWOT).[23] For Bush, the GWOT provided both a solution to America's need for more oil and showed that its fight against *al-Qaida* had become worldwide. But it was a disaster for the Tuareg and other local peoples.

To return to the thirty-two hostages, President Bouteflika reportedly said at a conference in Austria in July 2003 that 'the hostages are in the hands of a terrorist group affiliated to Bin Laden's *al-Qaida*'.[24] Even before the hostages were released,

---

22   Salima Mellah writes that as early as March 2004, General Wald, of American forces in Europe (EUCOM), had recognised that *al-Qaida* members were trying to establish themselves in the Maghreb and the Sahel; this was constantly repeated but the Americans never questioned the reality that many witnesses maintained, that while the kidnappers were 'authentic kidnappers', the operation was organised by the *DRS*. *Algérie 2003 : l'affaire des "otages du Sahara", décryptage d'une manipulation,, http://www.algeria-watch.org/fr/aw/otages_sahara.htm, 22 septembre 2007.*

23   Keenan, 2013a, p 10 quoting Daniel Volman, 'The Bush Administration and African Oil: The Security Implications of US Energy Policy', *Review of African Political Economy (ROAPE),* Vol. 30, No. 98, Dec 2003, pp 573-84. The process of fracking, of producing oil and gas from shale, was perfected in the USA in the late 1990s. It has led to massive production in the USA so that oil and gas from overseas has hardly been required since that time.

24   *Le Jeune Indépendant*, 14 Jul 2003 (from ANH).

Washington was portraying the area as a new front in its Global War on Terror,[25] an area spreading from Mauritania across the wastelands where *El Para* had been – the Sahel – to Sudan, Somalia and across to Iraq and Afghanistan. US troops were dispatched to Mauritania in early 2004 and the US Under-Deputy of State said that Los Angeles-based contractors would assist. The US Air Force deputy commander with responsibility for most of Africa spoke of the Sahara as a 'swamp of terror' which 'we need to drain'. A curious turn of phrase for an area of the driest desert. The wildest accusations flew about: the region was (and is) a hotbed of Islamic terrorism with a*l-Qaida* bases deep in the desert. *El Para* and his 'terrorists' were supposedly responsible for bombings which had taken place in Tunisia, Casablanca, and Madrid;[26] there was a threat of 'terrorists' from Afghanistan and Pakistan 'swarming across the Sahel', and a danger of overthrow of the Algerian and Mauritanian governments...[27] The threats issued were literally terrifying.

Had a completely fictitious story of terrorism been built up to persuade the USA of the great friendship of the Algerian authorities, as has been suggested?[28] Indeed, Algeria is continually held up as the country that can teach the world so much about how to fight terrorism.[29] The *DRS* fed the USA with what it wanted – and not only did it do this, but it set up a real live piece of terrorism to back up its information. That real live piece of terrorism was the capturing of hostages by *El Para*, a most wanted 'terrorist'. But why was *El Para* never

---

25   The GWOT refers to the international military campaign that started after the 11 September 2001 attacks on the USA. George W Bush first used the term 'War on Terror' on 20 September 2001, 11 days after 9/11. This paragraph and that following are based on Keenan, 2013a, chapter 2.

26   This last refers to the bombing of trains in Madrid in March 2004 that killed 191 people and injured 1,800.

27   On 04 Jun 2005, an attack on Lemgheity barracks in Mauritania, claimed by *MBM* (*GSPC*) but manipulated by the *DRS* according to Géze & Mellah (2007), caused eighteen Mauritanian deaths.

28   Keenan, 2013a, p xi.

29   We have been told from time to time that senior US military leaders went to Algiers to learn about Algerian methods, including the use of torture.

brought before a court? It transpired[30] that he had indeed been captured in March 2004, in a 'fortunate manner' by a Malian group (the *MDJT*), who wanted to pass him to the Algerian authorities whatever the price; months later, in October, the Algerian Minister of the Interior announced that *El Para* had been extradited, not by a Mali group but by the Libyan authorities to the Algerian '*police judiciaire*'. He was then, in June 2005, tried *in absentia* (where had the Algerians allowed him to go?) and condemned to life imprisonment; he should have appeared again twice in 2007 and again in 2008 but by this time he was regarded as disappeared.

The sad result of this extraordinary story is that it has made what was a generally peaceable area, and one of the most beautiful places on earth, into one which has become very dangerous and where 'terrorist acts' have been on the rise, especially south of the Algerian border, since the early 2000s.

'TERRORISM' SPREADS FURTHER WITHIN THE SAHEL AND NORTH AFRICA

It has been noted that among the thirty-two tourists kidnapped in the Algerian Sahara in March-April 2003, a first group was released in May 2003, and a second group was taken on a roundabout route to Mali[31] and released in July. This seemed to be quite extraordinary, but we should have recognised that this had happened immediately before the USA invaded Iraq (20 March 2003) and some eighteen months after 9/11. It has already been noted that Washington was portraying the area as a new front in its GWOT, but some of us could not take these extraordinary comments seriously. We should have done, and noted more carefully the dispatch of US troops to Mauritania in January 2004. This almost unbelievable story, from the time

---

30   AW: *Où sont passés Hassan Hattab et Amari Saïfi alias Abderrezak El Para? 20 Dec 2008*.

31   Keenan 2009, p 72: 'We know from local people that Algerians, later identified as agents of Algeria's intelligence services, were active in northern Mali and preparing for the arrival of the hostages.'

of the kidnapping, had become deadly serious: George W Bush and his government were taking their GWOT to West Africa,[32] Bush identifying *El Para* as Osama Bin Laden's 'man in the Sahara'. US commanders, State Department and Pentagon officials emphasised the region as being an 'ungoverned area', not apparently thinking that of course nearly empty desert is quite naturally 'ungoverned' by western standards – it is largely populated by tribes living together in a way not understandable in western terms.

The US and Western intelligence-security forces, having linked the bombing of trains in Madrid and other atrocities in Tunisia and Morocco to *al-Qaida* groups in North Africa, warned of '*al-Qaida* bases hidden in the Sahara that could launch terrorist attacks on Europe.'[33] Donald Rumsfeld had, already in 2002, launched a 'Proactive, Preemptive Operations Group' called the P2OG, a covert organisation which would provoke 'terrorist' groups to undertake violent acts that would expose them to 'counterattack' by US forces in Bush's Pan-Sahel Initiative (PSI), or the 'American invasion' as the Tuareg and other local people called it.[34]

The day after the landing in Mauritania, a further 400 troops went to the Chad-Niger border, and a week later, announcements were made that most of the future work to be undertaken there would be going to civilian contractors.[35] This included the building of new bases; prior to this no nation in North or West Africa had allowed the US AFRICOM to build on their land.[36] An enormous base was started near Tamanrasset in the Algerian Sahara[37] for which a deep well was drilled to provide

---

32 General Jones had said "...we're going to have to go where the terrorists are." (Keenan 2013a p 16)
33 Keenan 2013a p 3.
34 Keenan 2013a p 14.
35 Including Halliburton.
36 As a result, AFRICOM, US Africa Command, had to be based in Stuttgart in Germany where it still is, many years later.
37 Keenan, 2013a, p 17: local people estimated its circumference to be of the order of 10 km and its runways approaching 4 km. Lodgings for 2,000 people had been built.

water; it dried up the wells of a local village, some 10 to 15 km away, and deprived the village of its water and livelihood. It did nothing for 'hearts and minds' about which the US makes such play. A political corruption scandal blew up in 2006 over the contractor Brown & Root Condor (BRC, owned by Halliburton) which meant that the base was never completed.[38] Local people were well aware of the chaos caused by US action in Iraq and elsewhere, and now it was affecting them. The Tuareg, fighting to retain their way of life, have been suffering particularly badly.[39] Anti-US sentiments have been driven by local people's anger at the impact of the US's GWOT; their anger is, however, more against their own regimes than Washington.[40] Nigerien troops,[41] trained by the US, have been responsible for appalling human rights abuses in Niger and a Nigerien government-directed 'ethnocide' against the Tuareg forced the Tuareg to take up arms...[42]

I shall not delve in detail into 'terrorism' in Mali and elsewhere in the Sahel: there have been a large number of attacks[43] with probably hundreds of deaths and a rash of radical groups, including Ansar Eddine,[44] *MUJAO, IS* and *AQMI*. Ancient manuscripts and buildings have been destroyed,[45] and there

---

38 Keenan, 2103a, pp 17-18.
39 Thousands of refugees have fled across the Sahara to Algeria and the rest of the Maghreb, trying to enter Europe.
40 Keenan, 2013a, p 28.
41 The term *nigérien* refers to the inhabitants of Niger; the spelling distinguishes them from Nigerians.
42 Keenan, 2009, p 209.
43 At least eighteen people were killed and 125 guests and thirteen employees were held hostage in an attack on a luxury hotel in the Malian capital Bamako in November 2015 (the *Independent*, 20 Nov 2015).
44 Emmanuel Macron, newly President of France, said when visiting Mali in May 2017 that he intended to speak very frankly with Algeria about Ag Ghali, creator of the 'jihadist' group Ansar Eddine and a pawn of the Algerian *DRS*.
45 The International Criminal Court sentenced an Islamist militant who destroyed ancient shrines in Timbuktu to nine years in jail. This was the first sentence based on cultural destruction as a war crime. http://www.bbc.co.uk/news/world-africa-37483967 Sept 2016. Thousands of priceless ancient manuscripts in Timbuktu were reported to have been destroyed by the Islamists, but later it was found that Malians had spirited most of their cultural legacy away so saving them (the *Independent* 26 Nov 2015).

have been kidnappings of foreigners and others.[46] Following a UN Security Council resolution in December 2012, France sent a 3,000-strong counter-terrorism deployment of French soldiers, together with fighter jets, helicopters and drones to the area.[47] It is a very complex situation: Wolfgang Lacher[48] writes that in the Sahel there are 'few alternative sources of income in the region and none... can rival the gains to be made from criminal activity'; organised crime, with state complicity, may have been the main factor enabling *AQIM*'s growth. There have always been local disputes, but these have become more serious now that arms traffickers have sold them arms and many join the 'jihadist groups' which are destabilising the region.[49] Thomas Miles also stresses the complexity of the situation in the Sahel but argues that today's crises are neither inevitable nor permanent.[50] Moussa Tchangari, a Nigerien analyst, writes of the 'war without end', of the corruption there, and that the majority of Sahel states, Mali in particular, have the greatest difficulty in maintaining their territorial integrity and are dependent on international 'guardianship'.[51]

Large numbers of people have migrated north across the Sahara over the years – and many have been sent back from Algeria under terrible conditions. The UNO Special

---

46   Foreigners killed or kidnapped included two Canadian UN diplomats close to Niamey in December 2008 and four tourists close to the Mali-Niger frontier in January 2010 – including a Briton, Edwin Dyer. The French launched a military operation to free seventy-eight-year-old Michel Germaneau but it led to the execution of the hostage; Spain obtained the release of two hostages for a ransom – according to *El Mundo* – of €4 million. Paying ransom has heavy consequences, providing an incentive for further kidnapping (this is why the UK government does not, in principle, pay ransoms) and no doubt accounts in part for why Edwin Dyer was executed, while two women with him and two Canadian diplomats were released after ransom payments. (Keenan, the *Independent*, 04 Jun 2009 *West's made-up terror links to blame for killing*)

47   This force was still there years later.

48   Lacher, W. 2012; Organized Crime and Conflict in the Sahel-Sahara Region. Washington, D.C.: Carnegie Endowment for International Peace. http://carnegieendowment.org/files/sahel_sahara.pdf

49   Rémi Carayol, *Le monde diplomatique, May 2017.*

50   This will appear in Miles' forthcoming book *The Sahel.*

51   *Sahel: aux origines de la crise sécuritaire.* Aug 2017.

rapporteur of Rights of Migrants demanded in October 2018[52] that the Algerian government cease the expulsion of Nigeriens immediately. Some had children at school, had worked and lived in Algeria for years and were woken and taken from their homes, without any belongings or clothes, to police stations where they were beaten and deported by bus to the Niger frontier, from where they had to walk. Algeria had expelled 35,000 Nigériens to Niger since 2014, he said.

Back in North Africa,[53] since the start of the so-called Arab Spring in late 2010 and early 2011, there have been a stream of allegations about the involvement of Algeria's *DRS* in trying to prevent the emergence of democratic governance in **Tunisia** but there was 'no hard evidence'. On 22 March 2015, four days after an attack on the Bardo Museum in Tunis where twenty-one European tourists were killed, Tunisia's new President, Beji Caid Essebsi, had said, visibly upset, in an interview with the French TV channel *I-Tele*: "Whenever a terrorist group is flushed out in Tunisia, it has an Algerian leader."[54] The Tunisian army had recovered mobile phones and SIM cards from the bodies of several Algerian 'jihadists' killed in the region. An analysis of the SIM cards by the Tunisian army revealed their communications with *DRS* officials in Algiers, including their phone numbers and even their nicknames. *AQIM*'s leader in the area, now dead, was Abdelhamid abou Zaïd, another *DRS* operative.

Those who do not consider seriously what Keenan writes, and dismiss him and others as conspiracy theorists or cranks, should look more deeply at the attack by 'terrorists' on the BP/Statoil In Amenas gas facilities in January 2013, and the independent revelations that Habib Souaïdia describes from

---

52   https://algeria-watch.org/?p=69641
53   State Crime Research, 8 Jul 2015. Habib Souaïdia and Algerian state crime. http://statecrime.org/state-crime-research/habib-souaidia-algerian-state-crime/
54   This meant, said Souaïdia in the same article, that the leader of the museum attack was Algerian.

personally known witnesses actually present at that attack.[55] Since that time, several other writers have written in similar vein about the area.[56] Revelations in Hillary Clinton's private email server that were published by Wikileaks in 2016 provide new information about the *DRS* and *al-Qaida* which must have been known to the US and British authorities.[57]

---

55 *Révélations sur le drame d'In-Amenas : trente otages* étrangers *tués par l'armée algérienne, au moins neuf militaires tués.* 11 Feb 2013. http://www.algeria-watch. org/fr/aw/souaidia_in_amenas.htm

56 Gèze and Mellah, 2007; John R Schindler http://nationalinterest.org/commentary/ the-ugly-truth-about-algeria-7146?; Prince, 2014. Hillary Clinton emails, http:// statecrime.org/state-crime-research/thank-you-hillary-secretary-clintons-emailgate-revelations-about-algerian-state-crimes/.

57 The emails, described by Keenan, (http://statecrime.org/state-crime-research/ thank-you-hillary-secretary-clintons-emailgate-revelations-about-algerian-state-crimes/ 21 Apr 2016) provide vital information about the 'terrorist' leader *MBM* and his secret agreement with the Algerian authorities, about an alleged *al-Qaida/ AQIM* training camp at Tamouret in the Sahara actually run by the *DRS*, and about Algeria's support for the Gadaffi regime in Libya following the 'Arab Spring' there in early 2011.

Tamouret camp's purpose was to press-gang, indoctrinate and train marginalised youths to commit atrocities in Algerian communities with whom they had no connection. The majority of youths were Algerian, but there were also nationals from Mauritania to the Horn of Africa, Central Asia and Afghanistan in the east. They were generally executed after they had performed their tasks, or before if they gave any hint of dissent – they were seen as 'utterly disposable'. Prisoners were to be killed as part of the training process and were delivered to the camp by the army/*DRS* on average four times a week; those killed included army officers and soldiers who had presumably stepped out of line or were deemed 'suspect', as well as 'civilians' or 'common criminals', from the prisons. These latter, Keenan believes, comprised many 'disappeared' from the 'dirty war' of the 1990s. The common form of killing was throat-slitting. Keenan states that it is inconceivable that American and British intelligence agencies, who were working with the *DRS*, did not know what was going on at the camp. Tamouret was the site of the cold-blooded murder of hundreds, if not thousands, of innocent victims. It appears to have been closed around 2009.

The emails say that Algeria would provide the US administration with information and operational assistance in its GWOT and in exchange the US would assist Algeria to re-equip its technologically run-down military forces.

DEADLY ATTACK ON BP SAHARA IN AMENAS GAS INSTALLATIONS –
SEVENTY-EIGHT KILLED? (JANUARY 2013)[58]

Algerian oil and gas facilities were never seriously attacked
during the years of violence from 1992 onwards.[59] It was said
that the *FIS* and opponents of the regime wanted to ensure
that oil and gas production would continue when they came to
power. That changed on 16 January 2013 when a group of about
twenty Islamic militants[60] attacked and temporarily seized the
natural gas facility 40 kms southwest of the town of In Amenas[61]
and 80 km from the Libyan border, and seized hostages. The
Algerian military then stormed the place: the result left nearly
eighty people dead, thirty-nine of whom were foreign nationals
from nine countries. The In Amenas facility is run jointly by
British Petroleum (BP) and Statoil (the Norwegian state oil
company) in conjunction with Sonatrach, and six Britons and
five Norwegians were killed.

The Algerian authorities released only minimum
information, much of which was unverifiable and almost certainly
'disinformation'.[62] An American writer, Rob Prince,[63] noted that both

---

58   Reports of the number killed have varied considerably. Perhaps the most recent
     report (In Amenas: Inquest Cover-Up and Western Involvement in Algerian
     State Crimes (*statecrime.org/data/.../KEENAN-IN-AMENAS-REPORT-FINAL-
     November-2016.pdf.*) stated that eighty people died, of whom thirty-nine were
     foreign nationals; they included ten Japanese, eight Philippinos, six British (plus
     one resident), five Norwegians, three Americans, two Romanians, two Malaysians,
     one French and one Colombian. Twenty-nine of the 'terrorists' were killed and
     nine or ten Algerians. Earlier numbers of reported deaths had been even higher:
     Prince 2014 reported 114.

59   There had been a couple of minor attacks on pipelines in the north in the 1990s.

60   Jon Marks, an Associate Fellow of the Royal Institute of International Affairs
     (Chatham House), in written evidence to the UK Parliament's Foreign Affairs
     Committee   (http://www.publications.parliament.uk/pa/cm201314/cmselect/
     cmfaff/86/86we03.htm) states (para 33) that the majority of the fighters came from
     Libya and Tunisia, not Algeria or Mali. He describes the group as 'a radical Islamist
     khatiba (battalion), Al-Mouakioune Bi Dam (The Blood Signatories)'.

61   The gas facility is also known as Tiguentourine.

62   *A New Phase in the War on Terror?* Keenan 2013b.

63   Prince, 2014.

Souaïdia[64] and Keenan[65] 'wrote damning critiques of the Algerian official explanations of In Amenas; both put together a substantial case suggesting that In Amenas was actually an inside job – a classic false-flag operation – managed and actually carried out by the *DRS* in order to make the Algerian security apparatus look good!'

The UK Prime Minister, David Cameron, made a 'working and friendship' visit to Algeria on 30 January 2013, two weeks after the attack. Articles in the Algerian press[66] wrote about what was expected to be discussed but not about what actually happened. *El Watan* wrote that several British newspapers said Cameron would propose aiding Algeria in tracking down the leader of the attack, *MBM*,[67] while *The Sun*[68] said that he would ask Algeria to authorise MI6 to seek the leader of *al-Qaida* and to play a part in the search for *MBM*. *Le Quotidien d'Oran* wrote that these requests would obviously be declined. Back in Britain, Jon Marks[69] provided Parliament's Foreign Affairs Committee with written evidence about what he calls 'the Malian intervention', discussing 'the role of key stakeholders in the region, with emphasis on Algeria.' He states (paragraph 12) that Algeria's *DRS* has 'long exerted influence over Mali and other Sahel states. This led to claims that the *DRS* had cultivated "jihadist" elements,[70] including *MBM*, as "assets" in their efforts

---

64 Habib Souaïdia, *Révélations sur le drame d'In-Amenas: trente otages étrangers tués par l'armée algérienne, au moins neuf militaires tués.* Algeria-Watch, 11 February 2013.

65 Jeremy Keenan, 2013b. *A New Phase in the War on Terror? International State Crime Initiative.* There is much here about collusion and about *MBM* and Mohamed Lamine Bouchneb; the general consensus, promoted by the Algerian authorities and seemingly accepted by virtually all the media, is that the mastermind of the attack was forty-year-old *MBM*, with Bouchneb being his key 'lieutenant' on the ground.

66 1) *El Watan, 31 Jan 2013, Au secours des intérêts britanniques.*
    2) Moncef Wafi, *Le Quotidien d'Oran, 31 Jan 2013, Cameron à Alger : une visite, un message.* http://www.algeria-watch.org/fr/article/pol/geopolitique/cameron_visite.htm

67 Hillary Clinton's emails as well as Keenan confirm that *MBM* was not present in the attack at In Amenas.

68 A British newspaper.

69 http://www.publications.parliament.uk/pa/cm201314/cmselect/cmfaff/86/86we03.htm.

70 I make the same comment about the 'jihadist' as I have for 'terrorist': since it is often unclear in what sense jihadist is used, I place it in inverted commas, except where it appears in a quote.

to control the region. The *DRS* has significant links to the region south of Algeria, but it has probably never been fully in control.'

Habib Souaïdia, in his paper about In Amenas published a month after the attack,[71] states that 'with rare exceptions' western media[72] simply repeated the information provided by 'anonymous security services', which provided no serious answers to what had really happened, how or why. Souaïdia's information came from well-informed witnesses: army patriots, which did not permit them to say exactly what had happened but allowed them to provide important unpublished information, particularly about dissensions among top military chiefs and about the heavy losses – never otherwise mentioned – among the ranks of the Algerian army. Souaïdia's paper asks two essential questions: i.) where did the terrorists come from? and ii.) why was this operation undertaken? On the first question, the Minister of the Interior 'affirmed' on 17 Jan (the day following the attack) that the group of thirty-two men from seven different countries came from Libya where it was formed and trained; after the formal Libyan denial the same day he said that it "appeared clearer that the group was an Islamist commando and that it had come from the north of Mali and it had taken two months to do so."[73] There are also doubts, says Souaïdia, about claims put out by the 'jihadist' *MBM*, described as a 'Bin Laden

71   Habib Souaïdia, *Révélations sur le drame d'In-Amenas: trente otages* étrangers *tués par l'armée algérienne, au moins neuf militaires tués.* Algeria-Watch, 11 February 2013. The whole of this paragraph is based on Souaïdia's paper.

72   *idem*: Two weeks after the attack, on 31 January, 145 strictly supervised Algerian and western journalists were on the site. This visit furnished no significant information: it was provided solely by officials from the regime and Algerian journalists who are notorious spokespersons from the *DRS* and *police politique*.

73   *idem*: this would have been a journey of 1,500 km within the Algeria Sahara – how could the group have escaped the Algerian security forces, present in large numbers and with significant surveillance systems? Souaïdia writes that the army had been reorganised so that one region (the 6th) was set up to better combat *AQMI* – in this region American experts had provided i) high-tech materials such as drones, planes and balloons, all equipped with sophisticated cameras and ii) expertise to *DRS* officers on how to counter efforts to destabilise the region. Considerable further information is provided by Souaïdia, concluding that it should have been very improbable that a terrorist commando could have penetrated a site 'in a zone better watched than that of the presidency of the Republic.'

of the desert' since 2005. He was targeting, he said, the Algerian regime for having allowed France to use Algeria's land and air space to kill 'ours' in Mali.

Souaïdia relates how things went wrong when the action against the gas facilities commenced: this was in part due to three different combat entities being used 'to liberate the hostages': 450 men against thirty-two terrorists.[74] He cites five generals among whom there was a struggle.[75] Dozens, especially foreigners, had been killed due to the decisions of Major-General Athmane Tartag to open fire, against the intention of the Commandant of the 4th Military Region, in which In Amenas is situated. Three M24 helicopters firing guided laser missiles killed eleven terrorists and the thirty hostages that they were detaining; Tartag once more ordered an M24 to fire, killing terrorists and their hostages and seven to ten soldiers and *gendarmes*. In reply to the government's public claim that the terrorists intended to blow up the gas facility, Souaïdia says that the terrorists were heavily armed but they did not appear to have the material to blow up the plant.

Souaïdia concludes his paper[76] by asking 'who profits from the crime?'… and why was the operation undertaken? He says that much is unknown about the attack, that much goes to suggest that the operation was controlled by radio by the *DRS*, but that he cannot be categorical about this. Other than the points he has already mentioned, including i) the difficulties of a commando force escaping Algerian surveillance in the Sahara and ii) the role of *MBM* and *AQIM* leaders, one has to ask about the strange relations that *DRS* chiefs have with different 'terrorist', 'Islamist'

---

74   Souaïdia wrote in this same paper: 'The Prime Minister announced that the elite unit of the ANP had done something that few comparable units in the world could have done: "freed hundreds of Algerian hostages" which Souaïdia says was far from the truth since the attackers had said they wanted foreigners and had "let hundreds of Algerians go free".'

75   General Tartag, who, the following year, replaced 'Tewfik' at the head of the *DRS*, apparently started this, calling Colonel Abdaoui 'son of a whore'.

76   Habib Souaïdia, *Révélations sur le drame d'In-Amenas: trente otages étrangers tués par l'armée algérienne, au moins neuf militaires tués*. Algeria-Watch, 11 February 2013.

and 'nationalist' groups in the Sahel. Men of the *DRS* continue to manipulate those in charge of these groups, he says.

The way that the *DRS* plays a double game of infiltrating and manipulating different armed groups recalls that of the Pakistani ISI (Pakistan Interservices Intelligence) with the Afghan and Pakistani Talibans.[77] One certainly cannot exclude that the *DRS* chiefs are able to manipulate a group of Islamists – whose head is one of their agents – and that this is done to demonstrate to the West that the Algerian army remains the best guarantor of their interests. On 24 Jan 2015, only a week after the attack, the British ambassador in Algiers, Martyn Roper, is reported to have said[78] that "the UK considers Algeria to be a key partner in the fight against terrorism." And François Hollande, President of France, said:[79] "We have need of Algeria in this region (Mali and the Sahel) for the struggle against terrorism and to favour a political dialogue including the Tuareg." For me, writes Souaïdia, there is no general staff in the army, there is the *DRS* which commands the army and

[77] John R Schindler (2012b) makes this interesting comparison: Pakistan's ISI and its appalling history has, it seems, never been well understood in the UK.

Schindler makes other pertinent comments about Algeria and the *DRS*. He writes: 'Years of U.S. investment in the region, especially expensive efforts by the Pentagon's Africa Command (AFRICOM) to build up Mali's security forces, have failed dismally.'

'After years of warnings by AFRICOM that jihadists threaten the Sahel, the U.S. solution, predicated upon training local forces to do the hard work, has been found wanting and the threat is now upon us. Yet how the DRS has done that is something which Washington seems reluctant to ask questions about. To be sure, its methods include tactics which the United States must be careful about associating itself with, including sponsoring terrorist groups and committing human rights abuses on an industrial scale.'

- 'Given how often over the past twenty years Western hostage dramas have been exploited by the Algerian regime –meaning the *DRS* – for political effect, it's time to start asking questions about what Algiers is really up to across the region. To what extent does the *DRS* continue to clandestinely support 'terrorism', as it did in the 1990s, as a weapon to discredit political Islam? It was a tactic that worked successfully but cost tens of thousands of civilian lives. There is ample evidence that the *DRS* maintains control of at least some of the jihadist bandit-groups operating under the rubric of Al-Qa'ida in the Islamic Maghreb (*AQIM*) across the Sahel.'

[78] Martyn Roper: *Nous allons tirer les leçons de cette attaque* , *Liberté*, 24 Jan 2013.

[79] Hacen Ouali: *Devant le Parlement européen. François Hollande affirme le rôle-clé de l'Algérie au Sahel*, El Watan, 6 February 2013.

which governs Algeria. How can we believe, for example, Major-General 'Bachar' Tartag, a torturer who, with his men, has eliminated thousands of persons in the torture center of Ben-Aknoun? It has been proved for a long time that the *DRS* undertakes 'terrorist' operations and protects key nebulous 'terrorist' elements.[80]

As usual, neither Souaïdia nor Keenan seemed to be taken seriously by the mainstream media in Europe or the USA at the time.[81] Rob Prince[82] wrote that 'The Algerian government immediately claimed that the attack was the work of Islamic fundamentalist radicals tied to or close to **al Qaida in the Maghreb (AQIM),** but how could a group of militants cross hundreds of miles of Sahara desert from Libya and/or Niger without detection?... The Algerian military presence in the region is significant and they pride themselves on their ability to protect oil and gas facilities.' He goes on to say that Hocine Malti, ex-Sonatrach vice president, stated that the USA and Britain, following an investigation by their intelligence services the CIA and MI6, demanded that, before restarting operations at the plant, the Algerian government undertake a major purge of high-ranking military and security personnel responsible for ensuring security at the base. France and Norway may also have been behind this demand. However it happened, between September 2013 and January 2014, most of the DRS's top generals were dismissed or 'retired'. The head of the *DRS*, 'Tewfik', 'managed to cling to his position' until September 2015.

In February 2015, there was an inquest in Britain into the

---

80 John R Schindler, 2012a: 'Most Western experts seem content to avoid any real discussion of the *DRS*, viewing it as a sort of myth or "conspiracy theory" which need not be considered.' http://nationalinterest.org/commentary/algerias-hidden-hand-7994

81 I should perhaps mention, in contradiction to nearly everything in this account, that Dalia Ghanem-Yazbeck, a research analyst at the Carnegie Middle East Center in Beirut, writes that 'In the region, there is only Algeria which is capable of combatting extremism and radicalism,' Hadjer Guenanfa, *Opérations militaires occidentales en Libye : quelles conséquences pour l'Algérie, TSA,* 03 Mar 2016.

82 Prince, 2014.

deaths of the British personnel killed at In Amenas. Relatives of those killed had expected that this would expose the truth of what had happened. The coroner concluded 'that they had been unlawfully killed' and that, 'Responsibility for the deaths lay with the terrorists… even though they were reported killed by Algerian army bullets in the subsequent rescue operation.'[83] The same article states that, 'Key documents and forensic records have been denied to the inquest because the Algerian authorities are putting on trial several alleged militants who survived the attack' and that, 'the Foreign Office resorted to the rarely used legal device of a public interest immunity (PII) certificate, allowing officials to apply to withhold material deemed too sensitive to be released in open court.' This meant that the report excluded evidence about the UK's awareness of the DRS's and Algeria's involvement in the attack. Too many questions had again arisen.

Prince concludes by asking if 'the whole incident was (not) contrived, planned and executed by the *DRS*, with its long and sordid history of false flag operations? To outsiders, it all sounds bizarre, incomprehensible, bordering on the conspiratorial, if not downright "over the top". To Algerians, on the contrary, it was all quite reasonable, the way things have been done in the country for decades.'[84]

83   The *Guardian*, 26 Feb 2015: *In Amenas murders: coroner points to security flaws at Algerian gas plant.*
84   *Huffpost Algérie* (27 February 2015) wrote that a London judge had stated that the responsibility for the death of six Britons 'killed illegally' is 'attributable to terrorists' even if two were killed by Algerian army bullets in the course of freeing the hostages. http://www.algeria-watch.org/fr/article/mil/*groupes_armes/enquete_ In Amenas.htm*

9

THE END OF AN ERA? 'TEWFIK' DISMISSED, BOUTEFLIKA RESIGNS AND MILLIONS DEMAND CHANGE

By the early 21st century some of the 'old guard' of the *DRS* was dying out or being replaced, but not by the younger generation of senior officers. Mohamed Lamari, regarded by many as the real power in the early 1990s, had quite unexpectedly resigned in 2004[1] and was replaced by Gaïd Salah – another of the 'old generation'. Mohamed Lamari died in 2004 and was thus able to escape arrest and judgement for his part in the 'dirty war', as was Smaïn Lamari, who died in August 2007. Will 'Tewfik' and others also be able to escape prosecution and justice?

Early in 2013, Amar Saâdani, the Secretary General of the *FLN*, vehemently attacked 'Tewfik', whom he accused of being behind attempts at destabilisation aimed at the *FLN* and the

---

1   Bouteflika, supported by other 'deciders'… successfully isolated the powerful Lamari and Nezzar. Riccardo Fabbiani. *The Changing Nature of the Algerian Political System and the Illusion of a Civilian Regime.* Jadaliyya Interviews, 06 Aug 2015.

Prime Minister.² He also said that he could not understand why the *prefets* of the *wilayas* and the heads of businesses should be controlled by colonels and their phone lines tapped. He then went on to say that the *DRS* had failed in providing protection to President Boudiaf, to the monks of Tibhirine, to oil and gas bases in the Sahara and to many others. All this, he said, is done under the orders of 'Tewfik' and he should resign. Saâdani's attacks caused a hue and cry, and the Algerian newspapers were full of it for many days. Several politicians and army officers claimed that the 'Bouteflika clan' was behind Saâdani making these comments, and accused the clan of wanting to weaken the *DRS*.

The continuity of the regime had been assured by the power of the *DRS* and its Head, 'Tewfik', for twenty-five years. Some other leading figures seem to have had very little power at all. And then, two and a half years later, following the 'retirement' of many very senior officers, on 13 September 2015, 'Like a clap of thunder from the sky… the presidence of the Republic announced that it had… today "dismissed" Mohammed Médiène ('Tewfik') from his post of Head of the *DRS*.'³ He was seventy-six years old and had been the strong man of the Algerian economy and politics for the past twenty-five years. He had been the principal organiser of the strategy of counter-insurrectional war and of state terrorism, which caused tens of thousands of deaths and forced disappearances from 1992 to the early 2000 years, and it was said that he was the principal designer of *la machine de mort*, the torture 'death machine'. He was replaced by Athmane Tartag (sixty-five), known as 'Bachir'. International media followed the thesis of most of the Algerian press – that this move was prior to Saïd Bouteflika, younger brother, replacing the President. The Algerian media concluded that the eviction of 'Tewfik' marked the triumph of the 'Bouteflika clan' over 'Tewfik' and his clan.

2   TSA, 13 Feb 2013.
3   'De 'Tewfik' à Tartag : un criminel contre l'humanité en remplace un autre à la tête des services secrets algériens. http://www.algeria-watch.org/fr/aw/de_Tewfik_a_tartag.htm

There are, however, good reasons for not reaching this conclusion. Algeria-Watch has received much information from reliable witnesses which has not otherwise been made public, from patriotic officers who are revolted by what their superiors do or have done, and from others.[4] This information can be verified and validated, permitting AW, which does not agree with the thesis of the struggle between the two clans, to shine a light on what it concludes are the true reasons for the 'departure' of 'Tewfik'. Athmane Tartag, who replaced 'Tewfik', had been one of the worst offenders as part of 'Tewfik's *machine de mort,* where thousands were tortured and killed. AW describes the background and history of 'Tewfik' and Tartag and the state terror and the crimes against humanity which it is claimed they instigated. Witnesses include Mohammed Samraoui, who tells us that when he himself was in the *DRS* (he was a colonel), he visited Tartag, who had formerly been his friend and subordinate, and found that he had completely changed. It was astounding, he said. Tartag told him that he had formed, on the orders of his chief, and from as early as 1992, 'commando' units, which were charged not only with executing suspects but also with terrorising families of Islamists. The units were sent in the middle of the night to selected families who were living in 'Islamist' areas; the 'commandos' would bang on the doors, shouting "We are *mujahideen,*" and when the door was opened they would massacre the family. These actions served primarily to terrorise the population. "Tartag was no longer the gentle, obliging, educated, human man I had known. In front of me was Lt Col Tartag, who had become a monster."[5]

Why had Tartag replaced Médiène? AW reviews what the francophone Algerian press wrote over the previous two years (2013-15) when the *DRS* was gradually weakened and it followed that 'Tewfik' (Médiène) should officially depart. It further asks: can one really pretend, as does most of the Algerian media, that

4   *De 'Tewfik' à Tartag* : un criminel contre l'humanité en remplace un autre à la tête des services secrets algériens.
5   Algeria-Watch has abstracted this from Samraoui 2003b, pp. 199-200.

it was a 'vast operation led by the presidential clan to destroy the *DRS*'? AW admits that the information given is incomplete and sometimes contradictory but that, after taking out the pure propaganda, and considering significant information that was not published, a much more likely picture than that of a struggle between two clans emerges. The significant pieces of information missing were:

- The background to the killing of many of the hostages on the gas site of Tiguentourine[6] in 2013 was revealed by Habib Souaïdia. He wrote that 'according to well informed military patriots' who were present at the site, Tartag had given the order to men commanded by General Hassan 'to fire in a group': the missiles fired by their helicopters had without distinction killed both Islamist terrorists and western hostages whom they were detaining.
- Secondly, Souaïdia concluded that the western secret services, MI6 (UK), CIA (USA) and *DGSE* (France), would have known very quickly who had killed their citizens, but this knowledge had to be hidden from the *DRS* since they were collaborating together on 'anti-terrorism'.[7] However, furious about the *DRS* crime, the American and British secret services made known that such a thing must never happen again, and this led to the eviction of Major-Generals Athmane Tartag and M'henna Djebbar from their posts. But why then should the Americans accept three years later that Tartag should replace 'Tewfik'? According to AW's best sources, it was due to the double game that the Americans (and their European partners) were playing in trying to conceal the role

---

6   See in Chapter 8: *Deadly attack on BP Sahara Tiguentoutine gas facilities – seventy-eight killed.*

7   The Americans have for many years applauded, and sought advice from, the *DRS* about tackling 'terrorism'.

of the *DRS* chiefs in organising 'Islamist violence', while at the same time making it known to them that they must stop this practice. 'Tewfik's replacement by Tartag would protect 'Tewfik' because Tartag had been his accomplice since 1992.

• For Algeria-Watch, the nomination of Tartag to head the *DRS* does not in any way presage the end of the Bouteflika regime. The system remains in place, free from any democratic control, and the Americans, having been complicit in a number of actions in the Sahel attributed to 'Islamists', also want to avoid any major scandal. It is also a system designed to maintain absolute control of the *rente*[8] and of the country's income. However, Mohamed Samraoui had said in an interview in 2014[9] that the *DRS* no longer had the power that it had the previous year and that the new generation of generals are more responsible and more mature.

However one may view the dismissal of Tartag and the earlier resignation of Mohamed Lamari in 2004, there have been profound changes, and the *DRS* as such no longer exists, having been broken up in September 2015. The small circle of controlling military and civilians, noted for their opacity, is threatened by businessmen and others connected to the military who have no loyalty to those who fought in the War of Independence and are only interested in their personal fortunes. But it cannot be concluded that the military does not continue to have the greatest influence, at least until 2019, in what is happening in Algeria. It is still the most stable and best organised institution in

8   *La rente*, private income, is the term used for the enormous income which comes from the export of oil and gas. Luis Martinez has written in *Violence de la rente pétrolière (Presse de sciences Po, 2010)* that the regime has transformed itself into a predatory business and has become a bazaar and *rente* economy.

9   *TSA*, 09 Feb 2014 *http://www.algeria-watch.org/fr/article/pol/anp_presidence/samraoui_itv.htm*. This is an important paper, where Samraoui, the author of *Chronique des années de sang*, is interviewed by a TSA journalist.

the country; for the military leaders, abandoning their political role and leaving the country in the hands of civilians could put the nation in danger.[10]

There has been much written in English about the horrors of *la sale guerre* but there seems to be little consensus view, except that it has been such a complex situation and that atrocities were carried out by 'Islamists', which as I have stated is at least in part true. I conclude that more than enough has been published in the French language, particularly by Algerians, to make plain that the Algerian Security Services (the *SM/DRS*), headed by 'Tewfik' from 1990 to 2015, have been responsible for manipulating, if not directly responsible for, many of the major atrocities that have taken place during those twenty-five years.

QUESTIONS ABOUT THE PRESIDENCY AND THE POWER OF THE ALGERIAN STREET

The Secretary General of the *FLN*, Djamel Ould Abbes, announced on 28 October 2018, to general surprise, that the profoundly disabled Abdelaziz Bouteflika was the *FLN* candidate for the 2019 presidential elections, scheduled to take place on 18 April.[11] Two weeks later, Ould Abbes resigned 'for health reasons' and 'the political sky trembled again'. Then, in December, it was announced that the elections would be delayed a month or would not take place and that there would be a revision of the constitution.[12] On 22 February 2019, and on succeeding Fridays and Tuesdays, hundreds of thousands, and up to millions,[13] of people have come peacefully onto the streets and onto balconies all over Algeria, firstly to reject the proposal that a permanently incapacitated man should be re-elected President for a fifth term. In addition

10 Dalia Ghanem Yazbeck. *La succession dépendra du modus vivendi entre le clan Bouteflika et les militaires.*
11 https://algeria-watch.org/?p=69882.
12 *Le Soir d'Algérie, 16 dec 2018 L'élection présidentielle n'aura pas lieu* https://algeria-watch.org/?p=70412
13 https://algeria-watch.org/?p=73058; 'a number never seen before'.

to their Wednesday assembly, families of *SOS Disparus* actively joined the marches, where they called for truth and justice. On 12 March, President Bouteflika sent a message announcing the postponement of the elections and renouncing his bid to seek a fifth term as President,[14] and on 2 April he resigned.

The army commanders – who determined that Bouteflika should be president for a fifth term and got it wrong – were now faced with a massive dilemma: the people, especially the young, were challenging the generals' hegemony over the state. The demonstrations have united the Algerians as never before, but the popular movement has no explicit leaders who negotiate on its behalf. 'Sticking to its peaceful strategy and perhaps also accepting the satisfaction of its immediate demand as the basis for further claims later, while preserving its own unity, may be the wisest course.'[15]

Wealthy businessmen and others left, or tried to leave, with hoards of cash, by air or by road. The police at airports and frontiers have listed more than 500 people who are forbidden to leave the country but some have already escaped. Ahmed Ouyahia, four times prime minister, was barred from leaving the country, while others have been caught at borders escaping with their families and huge sums of cash. Private planes are not allowed to land in the country.

The people are calling for change, the Algerian state is in crisis and the generals and others are faced with the people challenging them and their control of the state. Gaïd Salah, army Chief of Staff and regarded as the strong man of the country for fifteen years,[16] had called for the application of Clauses 7 and 8 of the Constitution which referred to the sovereignty of the people, and this had given them hope. And then the bombshell fell.[17] On 9 April, Abdelkader Bensalah was appointed the new Head of State for ninety days, and both the Minister of the

14   Algerian Embassy, Oslo, 12 Mar 2019.
15   Roberts, *Algeria rising*, 15 Mar 2019, AW.
16   He died suddenly on 23 Dec 2019.
17   Makhlouf Mehenni, TSA, 09 Apr 2019, https://algeria-watch.org/?p=71805

Interior and the minister who will direct the electoral process were appointed. In the streets, police used water cannons and tear gas. But this has in no way stopped those marching every Friday. In 'grossly fraudulent'[18] elections on 12 December 2019, 'where nothing has changed', and when less than 40% of the population voted, one of the elderly candidates, Abdelmadjid Tebboune, was appointed 'President'.

Nassera and others are most hopeful that the marches of young people and others will end by bringing change. To return to my main human rights concern, is it possible that families of the disappeared, and others who suffered so terribly and tragically under the regime, may now be able to look forward to the day when their efforts to obtain truth and justice will be successful?

---

18   https://algeria-watch.org/?p=73073

10

IS TRUTH AND JUSTICE POSSIBLE FOR FAMILIES OF THE DISAPPEARED?

Many years ago, I visited the Holocaust Museum in Washington DC: as one left the museum up the escalator, on the wall in large letters was written something along the lines of: *What you have seen is displayed so that it will never occur again.* I wish I had written the phrase down, because it has haunted me ever since. And what is disturbing is that it is still going on. It is not just a museum to something that happened once, in the 1940s. It is indeed occurring, every day – not, happily, in the same number – although in Rwanda more people were killed in a year than in any year during the holocaust. What I see is that every person disappeared, tortured or killed without trial, is a human being, a tragedy, a loved one.

And what are we doing about it? AI becomes involved in international criminal courts investigating crimes against humanity, and we, individual members, write letters, to a prisoner or relatives of killings, torture and enforced disappearances.

CRIMES AGAINST HUMANITY - CAN STATES AND INDIVIDUALS BE
HELD RESPONSIBLE?

In order to look at what is happening at the international level,
it is helpful to go back into a certain amount of history. We can
lay the blame for the way people have been treated by states
very much at the door of the concept of the Divine Right of
Kings, which imposed unquestioning obedience to the Prince.[19]
From this flowed a number of legal consequences, including
immunity from prosecution of heads of state. The power of the
divinely approved ruler over all of his or her subjects followed,
and this was challenged, for the first time ever, in Nuremberg
in 1945-6, as a result of the horrors of the Second World War
holocaust. From this followed a desire that it should not occur
again, which led to the **United Nations Declaration of Human
Rights** being adopted on 10 December 1948 by the UN General
Assembly.[20] The idea that citizens should have the right to be
protected from being tortured by the state then came up for the
first time. Pious comments were made by governments, but it
suited none of the five members of the Security Council[21] that
an individual should have rights in international law, so that
the Declaration was in no way legally binding.[22] It is only in the
21st century, and primarily spurred on by atrocities in South
America under dictators such as Pinochet in the 1970s and
'80s, the genocide in Cambodia in the 1970s and the wars in
ex-Yugoslavia in the 1990s, Rwanda and others, that there has
been a move towards international courts. **The International
Criminal Court** is a permanent international court established

19 Robertson, 1999, p 2f, 351ff.
20 It has since been reliably estimated that the number of victims of Stalin's purges
in the Soviet Union outnumbered the six million Jews lost in the Holocaust
(Robertson 1999 p 17).
21 USA, UK, France, USSR/Russia, China.
22 "Count up the results of fifty years of human rights mechanisms… and endless high
level rhetoric and the general impact is quite underwhelming… this is a failure of
implementation on a scale that shames us all." (Mary Robinson, UN Human Rights
Commissioner, 10 Dec 1998)

in 2002 to investigate, prosecute and try individuals accused of committing the most serious crimes: the crime of genocide, crimes against humanity and war crimes. It has the jurisdiction to prosecute individuals for these international crimes and only replaces national courts when these are unwilling or unable to prosecute or when the United Nations Security Council or individual states refer situations to the Court. Not only has the International Court been established but after many years, the question of 'disappearance' is no longer, in the second decade of the 21st century, a taboo subject in Algeria – there have been, and continue to be, frequent articles sympathetic with mothers and relatives of the disappeared in Algerian newspapers. Despite all the threats and intimidation and elderly men and others being beaten up, some severely, and taken to the police station and charged, demonstrations continued in front of the 'human rights' building and in the centre of the city at *la grande poste*. The *SOS disparus* offices have survived, despite not being legally recognised: they are places where families can meet and receive support. What are the chances of mothers and relatives of enforced disappearances obtaining what they most aspire to – truth and justice?

What were, and are now, needed are serious court inquiries into what happened in Algeria from 1992 onwards. An opportunity had occurred which would have provided much evidence in the western province of Relizane, where there had been hundreds of killings and many 'disappearances' in the mid-1990s. In December 2003, it was announced that a mass grave containing the remains of many people had been discovered. Among several other pieces of evidence, a pair of trousers and a cigarette lighter were identified by a local family as belonging to their disappeared relative. This would have been the opportunity to investigate the deaths.[23] An inquiry was promised but when investigators arrived, the remains had

---

23 'Les terrifiants massacres de Relizane, Dec 97-Jan 1998, Alg-Watch, 04 Jan 2016. http://www.algeria-watch.org/fr/aw/massacres_relizane.htm It was reported that many of those found dead had been buried alive.

themselves disappeared; this was clearly done in an attempt to conceal or destroy evidence; it also prevented relatives from the long-awaited chance to bury the victims in a dignified fashion.[24] Among many others – 120 police officers, according to *El Watan* – two mayors were arrested, perhaps the only time that this ever happened; they had reportedly subjected the local population to a reign of terror for five years. The two mayors were quickly released: a week earlier, in a programme made in 1996 on armed militia, these two mayors had been shown on Algerian television for 'their zeal, nationalism and competence'.

I am not aware of any other such opportunity for inquiry except for the burial of what may have been murdered civilians and prisoners at '**Tamouret**' SW of Illizi in the far south of the Sahara, evidence of which came to light in 2015.[25] Jeremy Keenan believes[26] that many of those buried there could have been disappeared people: he states that 'some of these graves have now been located and investigated, with the dead bodies and skeletal remains (along with accompanying data and evidence) being recorded photographically.'[27] I arranged a meeting for Nassera to come and meet Keenan in London, but Nassera concluded that there is little that can be done: security means that Tamouret is quite impossible to reach, we cannot have access to witnesses and having seen the photos, in comparison with what she has seen in Bosnia and Argentina, that the photographs of remains of bones which Keenan showed us are too old to have come from the years 1990. Despite this, however, Nassera believes that this is still a path to be followed since "as we say in France, there is no smoke without fire."

24 Amnesty International *Steps towards change or empty promises?* (16 Sept 2003 – AI Index: MDE 28/005/2003) and Press Release 9 Feb 2004 – AI Index MDE 28/001/2004.
25 Hillary Clinton's private email server iemails (http://statecrime.org/state-crime-research/thank-you-hillary-secretary-clintons-emailgate-revelations-about-algerian-state-crimes/). Hillary was US Secretary of State at the time.
26 Based on the evidence of a witness named 'Bashir'.
27 See http://statecrime.org/state-crime-research/thank-you-hillary-secretary-clintons-emailgate-revelations-about-algerian-state-crimes/ (3.ii. Confirmation of the existence of the Al Qaeda/DRS terrorist training camp)

A more promising line that can be followed when this becomes possible is through investigation of what are called '*tombes sous X*', those where the dead have been buried without having been identified before burial. Hacène Ferhati, a member of *SOS disparus* Oran, had said, in a meeting about disappearance and torture, that Farouk Ksentini, President of the *CNCPPDH*, had reported that there were 3,300 *tombes sous X*; these, Ferhati said, must be investigated and the bodies identified. The meeting was held in order to continue to struggle against 'forgetfulness' and to maintain pressure on the authorities to move towards 'a true civil concord, exposing the truth.'[28] The matter of torture was also brought up, 'since torture still goes on in our country' and one must not think it only happened in the past.

Nassera and a number of mothers of the disappeared visited Geneva 4-5 July 2018 when the **UN Human Rights Committee** (HRC) was considering the fourth periodic report presented by the Algerian government on human rights.[29] The UN committee experts were very concerned about a number of matters including 'the strong power of the executive branch (which) appointed all magistrates', the State's 'draconian restrictions on the right to peaceful demonstration' and that 'confessions obtained through torture were not strictly prohibited'. They asked the Algerian delegation to describe measures that were being taken about these and other human rights concerns. Lazhar Soualem, Permanent Representative of Algeria to the UN at Geneva, in his concluding remarks, explained that there were numerous projects under way in Algeria which would address many of the issues raised by the Committee. The Algerian government must reply within a year to serious observations made by the HRC. Will they?

Nassera was very positive about the meeting, and delighted that she and the mothers were able to present their case to UN representatives before the main meeting. Algeria,

---

28   D Loukil, *Liberté* 1 Jul 2018 *Les familles réclament l'identification des tombes sous X*
      https://algeria-watch.org/?p=68444

29   *http://www.algerie-disparus.org/lexamen-de-lalgerie-par-le-comite-des-droits-de-lhomme-des-nations-unies/*

being a signatory to the Geneva Conventions of 1960 and the International Covenant on Political Rights and the Torture Convention in 1989,[30] has a well-defined duty to look into potential violations, and under international human rights law a nation that has signed these agreements is obliged to uphold them or to let international actions against them take place. However, that doesn't happen. 'Obeisance to member state sovereignty is the United Nation's systemic defect,' and accounts for the Human Rights Committee being a toothless tribunal.[31] However, with the arrival of the International Criminal Court in 2002 and what has happened more recently, there are grounds for hope for families of the disappeared around the world.

HOW HAVE 'CRIMES AGAINST HUMANITY' BEEN TAKEN UP IN OTHER COUNTRIES?

How have disappearance, torture and other crimes against humanity been taken up elsewhere, and can those in Algeria seeking justice and truth learn from them?

In **Argentina,** a military dictatorship that had ruled the country from 1976 to 1983 was responsible for the disappearance, torture and murder of 15,000 to 30,000 people. In late 1983, three days after his inauguration, newly democratically elected President Alfonsin initiated legal proceedings against nine senior military officers leading to what was called the **Trial of the Juntas.** Five of the generals were sentenced to imprisonment and four were acquitted.

In **Morocco,** 300 prisoners were released in 1991 after being held in secret detention for up to nineteen years in appalling conditions. This was the climax of a long and energetic campaign by AI[32] and shows that prisoners who have been disappeared for years may still be alive.

---

30 These were signed under the presidency of Chadli.
31 Robertson, 1999, p xix.
32 Power, p 198.

More than twenty governments around the world have preferred **truth commissions** as a way to peace.[33] The **South African Truth and Reconciliation Commission** in 1995 was so successful precisely because it investigated politically motivated gross human rights violations: its intent was to prevent such atrocities from reoccurring. It was not perfect, but it was a very good start. There are other countries that have done nothing, and this includes Algeria. Who is going to take action against the nations that do nothing?

THE INTERNATIONAL CRIMINAL COURT

It had not been until fifty years after the 1940s Nuremburg trials that there was a genuine desire to put human rights at the centre of a 'New World Order'[34] and the **International Criminal Court (ICC)** was set up in The Hague in 2002 to prosecute individuals accused of committing the most serious crimes of concern to the international community: the crime of genocide, crimes against humanity and war crimes. This happened largely through the desire that something should be done following the crimes committed in South America in the 1970s and '80s under leaders such as Pinochet, the genocide in Cambodia under Pol Pot and what happened in ex-Yugoslavia in the 1990s. In 1999, 120 nations supported the Rome Statute for an International Criminal Court to be set up.[35]

Robertson[36] describes in considerable detail what happened in South America and the ex-Yugoslavia which helped legal conclusions to be reached from which the ICC could learn. Some of these are:

33   Le Sueur, 2010 pp 205-6.
34   Robertson, 1999, p xv.
35   Robertson, 1999, p 226.
36   Robertson, 1999, Chapters 7 to 10; note that the book was published in 1999, well before the Court was set up (2002).

- States which pardon torturers before a trial has taken place are in breach of their obligations.
- Every state has the power to pardon those who break its laws, but an amnesty may not be granted when the deeds are done at the behest of the state itself, which is what happened in Algeria. The Charter for Peace and National Reconciliation, which had given hope to millions of Algerians wanting the violence to end, had also given impunity to the military, the *gendarmes* and the police who had been involved in crimes against humanity. However, this was contrary to the obligation of the state to investigate and punish human rights violations and was a violation of the rights of relatives of the disappeared.[37]
- New governments cannot grant amnesties at the insistence of, say, the military or police.
- There is now, in international law, a duty on states to punish crimes against humanity, but in international practice, as in Algeria, where there have been thousands of such crimes (disappearance, torture, massacres), there has been a failure to do any such thing.
- One of the results of this is that crimes against international law may be punished by any state which obtains custody of persons suspected of responsibility, and this is what has happened in Switzerland, where Khaled Nezzar, as head of the army, has been brought before a court by three Algerian citizens who suffered torture at that time.

A major hurdle for Algerian families of the disappeared is that crimes against humanity committed before 2002 when the International Criminal Court was set up (2002) lie outside its jurisdiction.

---

37 Uruguay approved a referendum but it could not use the excuse that it expressed the will of the Uruguayan people (Robertson p 243).

RECENT SUCCESSFUL JUDGEMENTS

In May 2016, two remarkable international court judgements took place and two dictators were found guilty, not through the International Criminal Court but through **national courts**.

On 30 May 2016, **Argentina**'s last dictator, Renaldo Bignone, who had defended his actions as necessary in a 'battle against terrorism', was sentenced to twenty years in prison, decades after his role in hundreds of forced disappearances and other crimes, during the 1970s/'80s Operation Condor conspiracy to kill 'leftist' dissidents across South America and beyond.[38] Operation Condor had been carried out, in cahoots with the USA, by six South American dictators (Chile's Pinochet and the presidents of Argentina, Bolivia, Brazil, Paraguay and Uruguay). The major evidence came from US files, and a key piece of evidence was an FBI agent's cable that described the conspiracy in detail. So often, the only evidence in such cases is from families whose relatives have been killed or disappeared, and the US files were critical in reaching conviction.

Also on 30 May 2016, **Chad**'s former dictator, President Hissene Habré, was sentenced to life imprisonment by the Extraordinary African Chambers in Senegal.[39] So here is the case of a court in one country successfully prosecuting the former ruler of another. Habré was convicted of being responsible for thousands of deaths and torture atrocities in prisons between 1982 and 1990. The verdict demonstrates that where there is the political will, states and individuals can work together effectively to end impunity.[40] This was

---

38 The *Independent*, 8 Mar 2018. Bignone died in prison aged ninety. His crimes included the abduction of babies and the murder of purported subversives. He had orchestrated the shredding of documents that could implicate the *junta* in atrocities and declared a blanket amnesty covering military officials.

39 i newspaper, 30 May 2016 and https://www.amnesty.org/en/latest/news/2016/05/the-long-road-to-justice-for-chad-hissene-habre/)

40 Amnesty International, which, together with HRW and others, was involved in the case, described this as 'a great step forward for truth and justice'., (i newspaper, 30 May 2016) Sixteen other former military officers were also sentenced.

an extraordinary occurrence. Souleyane Guengueng[41] has described the terrible conditions in which he and others had been imprisoned in Chad in the late 1980s and how "From the depths of my cell, from the depths of that madness, I swore to fight for justice if I ever got out alive." Habré had lost the support of the USA and was overthrown in 1990; those in prison were freed. Guengueng and other victims and civil society groups then worked for more than twenty years and, in 2012, the African Union supported Senegal in clearing the way for justice to be done.

The case illustrates how victims of crimes against humanity can achieve justice, how the work of campaigners and human rights defenders really matters, and that heads of states and military commanders cannot expect to evade the net of international justice. It also illustrates how the African Union and civil society groups can be of assistance to other African countries where such crimes have been perpetrated.

In the late 1970s, perhaps 2 million were killed by the Khmer Rouge in **Cambodia**. Forty years later, when most of the other elderly Khmer Rouge leaders had died, two of them, aged ninety-two and eighty-seven, in the first genocide verdict of the UN-backed Tribunal in Cambodia, were convicted of genocide in 2018. A relative said "I am really satisfied with the sentences."[42]

ALGERIA AND BRINGING GENERALS TO JUSTICE

Turning back to Algeria, Khaled Nezzar, who was head of the army in 1988 when the military killed hundreds in Algiers, including children, had, in 2001, been flown to Algeria at midnight from Paris when three Algerians brought a suit against him for torture and other crimes. A year later, in 2002,

---

41   https://www.amnesty.org/en/latest/news/2016/05/the-long-road-to-justice-for-chad-hissene-habre/. https://fr.wikipedia.org/wiki/Souleymane_Guengueng and others.

42   BBC News, 16 Nov 2018. https://www.bbc.co.uk/news/world-asia-46217896

Nezzar had sued Habib Souaïdia in Paris over his book *La sale guerre* and lost his case. Then in January 2017, in Geneva, after five years, Nezzar was found not guilty, in two cases, of being responsible for war crimes brought before the *Ministère public de la Confédération (MPC)* by ex-members of the *FIS* through the Swiss NGO *TRIAL International*. The MPC had concluded there had been no armed conflict at the start of the 1990s and hence there could have been no war crimes. However, in May 2018, this was annulled by the Swiss TPF (*Tribunal pénal fédéral*), who recognised, in a fifty-page document, that a non-international armed conflict had indeed existed in Algeria at the start of the 1990s and that Nezzar was aware of the massive crimes committed under his orders and could not ignore the actions of his subordinates (including extrajudicial executions, forced disappearances and torture). The TPF therefore sent the case back to the MPC.[43]

Is there a possibility that DRS generals might be brought to trial before a national or international court? There are indications that courts, national and international, are becoming more able to deal with these situations than before the International Criminal Court was set up in 2002. It is recognised that where people are tortured, killed, or disappeared, there are ways of bringing those responsible to justice, and the prime way is through international instruments,[44] which do not allow those responsible to hide behind sovereign boundaries. It was this threat, and the possibility that it might lead to demonstrating French complicity with *le pouvoir* in Algeria, that caused the French to arrange a midnight flight from Paris that allowed General Khaled Nezzar to escape serious charges.

---

43   *Affaire Nezzar: Le tribunal pénal fédéral ordonne la reprise de l'instruction. Trial, 6jun18. AW 10jun18.*

44   The so-called 'Trial of the Juntas', the trial of members of the Argentinian government, including Jorge Rafael Videla, dictator of Argentina from 1976 to 1981, took place in 1985. Videla and Admiral Emilio Massera were sentenced to life imprisonment, others to some years of imprisonment. The trial was the only example of its type undertaken by a democratic government for many years. (Wikipedia: 'Trial of the Juntas', Nov 2016)

It was through being in Switzerland that Algerians there could bring him to court, and the Swiss TPF judgement is, surely, a very significant ruling. However, it raises the question as to how those, such as 'Tewfik' and senior members of the DRS who never leave Algeria, can be brought to trial. Are there any of the appointed judges in the country who would dare bring charges against them?

So, how can generals or ex-generals who never leave Algeria be brought to justice? As we have just seen, it has happened in Chad through the efforts of individuals and a coalition of NGOs, including AI, Human Rights Watch and the French *FIDH*.[45] AI, however, has not been able to visit Algeria for nearly twenty years, and Eric Goldstein, deputy Middle East and North Africa director at Human Rights Watch has said: "Since 2011, our organizations have regularly visited Morocco, Libya, and Tunisia with few if any obstacles… Algeria remains the only country among its neighbors that generally restricts access to human rights organizations."[46] As I have noted, there are also a number of significant Algerian human rights NGOs besides *SOS disparus,* including *LADDH, LADH* and *RAJ*,[47] which can raise their concerns about human rights infringements within the country. Perhaps a time could come, and it may be not so far distant, when NGOs are able to work together, re-engage in the crimes against humanity that have been committed in Algeria and assist Nassera and the mothers and relatives of those who are still fighting for truth and justice after so many years.

Le pouvoir is doing what it can to ensure that nothing changes, but we should note that 55% of young people in Algeria are under the age of thirty, many are unemployed and they are looking for

---

45   *Fédération internationale de ligues des droits de l'homme.*

46   *L'Algérie est le seul pays de la région qui bloque systématiquement les visites des ONG.* (Algeria is the only country in the region that systematically blocks visits of NGOs.) *El Watan 15 Nov 13.*

47   *Le Rassemblement Action Jeunesse (RAJ).* An NGO of active young people.

any sort of change to give them some hope for the future.[48] The terrible time of the 1990s was not part of their lives and they want a future and they want change in Algeria, as demonstrated by the remarkably peaceful marches that began on 22 February 2019. Could they be part of bringing about an end to military rule and bringing about democracy, and truth and justice for the mothers of the disappeared?[49]

We shall only have justice when all men, women and children are treated equally. When the USA and the UK face international courts over what happened in Afghanistan, Iraq and Syria, the UK in Northern Ireland and elsewhere in the last fifty years.[50] When individuals of whatever nationality, whatever

---

48   https://www.fidh.org/en/region/north-africa-middle-east/algeria/14629-algeria-allow-rights-groups-to-visit

As a member of the UN Human Rights Council, Algeria has pledged to cooperate with regional and international human rights organisations, but the Algerian authorities have not agreed to visits by the UN Special Rapporteur on Torture and the Working Group on Enforced or Involuntary Disappearances, despite their repeated requests, said Philip Luther, Middle East and North Africa director at Amnesty International… Algerian authorities have refused to grant visas to international human rights nongovernmental organizations for several years, and have violated in many ways the right of Algerian human rights organizations to operate freely. "Algeria remains the only country among its neighbors that generally restricts access to human rights organizations," said Eric Goldstein, deputy Middle East and North Africa director at Human Rights Watch. "Since 2011, our organizations have regularly visited Morocco, Libya, and Tunisia with few if any obstacles."

The groups that are making the appeal to the Algerian government to allow human rights groups access to the country include Amnesty International, Euro-Mediterranean Human Rights Network, Human Rights Watch and the Observatory for the Protection of Human Rights Defenders, a joint program of the International Federation for Human Rights (FIDH) and the World Organization Against Torture (OMCT).

"Algeria should end the farce of refusing any scrutiny of its own human rights record while sitting on the UN Human Rights Council," said Karim Lahidji, president of the FIDH.

49   A group of young people from different backgrounds announced that it was forming a political movement aspiring to change. *Maghreb Emergent 12 jan 2019.* https://algeria-watch.org/?p=70677

50   The UK has so far escaped having to appear before an international court for what appear to be valid claims of rendition and torture arising from the wars in Afghanistan and Iraq, and for its use of torture in Northern Ireland in the 1970s and '80s. The Prime Minister David Cameron had said, when he first heard about what happened in Northern Ireland, that there must be an inquiry. He said the same in 2010 about Iraq. But neither happened.

race, whatever religion, however highly placed, are tried and condemned openly and equally if they behave abominably to others, then we shall start to have justice. And out of justice comes peace. That is something worth working for, something to provide hope. In the meantime, some of us continue to work for those individuals who have been tortured, unjustly killed or imprisoned, for families of those who have disappeared. It is a small thing, but it also, in its own way, provides hope.

POSTSCRIPT

It is now just a year since Algeria erupted, on 22 February 2019, in a series of peaceful, twice-weekly marches and demonstrations all over the country, with up to millions of people, primarily young, known as *le Hirak* ('the movement'), calling for change. And change there has been. Bouteflika was forced to resign, his younger brother Saïd and other powerful businessmen, politicians, ministers and military were charged, many with corruption, tried and imprisoned. But some of the old hands, and the system itself, have remained. Gaïd Salah, Chief of Staff and *de facto* leader of the country, announced there would be new presidential elections to replace Bouteflika. Possibly as few as 10% of the electorate voted. Seventy-four-year-old Abdelmadjid Tebboune, who had been a Prime Minister in 2017, became President on 19 December and Gaïd Salah unexpectedly died of a heart attack four days later.

There are no leaders of *le Hirak*. It is a movement of the people and particularly of the young. They know that at present they cannot name a leader and that they have launched a movement that could go on for years.

In the meantime demonstrations, and many arrests, continue. But *le Hirak* remains and is determined to succeed in its struggle.

MAIN REFERENCES

Aggoun, Lounis and Jean-Baptiste Rivoire, 2004. *Françalgérie, crimes et mensonges d'Etats: histoire secrète, de la guerre d'indépendance à la <troisiéme guerre> d'Algérie. La Découverte, Paris.*

Algeria-Watch, 2003. *Algérie : la machine de mort.* Algeria-Watch, www.algeria-watch.org. (Report by Salah-Eddine Sidhoum and Algeria-Watch)

Algeria-Watch and Salah-Eddine Sidhoum, 2002. *Algérie: Les disparitions forcées en Algérie : un crime qui perdure.* Revised Jan 2007. Completed by Algeria-Watch Jan 2009, Jun-Jul 2012, 2014. Includes a list of all the known disappearances up to 2014.

Algeria-Watch, 2013. *Algérie 2012: Un régime de vieillards sanguinaires en fin de règne. http://www.algeria-watch.org/ fr/aw/fin_de_regne.htm.*

Algeria-Watch, 2015. *'De 'Tewfik à Tartag : un criminel contre l'humanité en remplace un autre à la tête des services secrets algériens'. https://algeria-watch.org/?p=45374 4 October 2015.*

Amnesty International, November 1993. Focus: Political Killings: Extrajudicial Executions/Excessive use of Lethal Force/

Deliberate and Arbitrary Killings by Armed Opposition Groups. Report 20426.

Amnesty International, November 1997. Algeria: Civilian population caught in a spiral of violence. Report 28/23/97.

Amnesty International, March 1999. *La fin du silence sur les 'disparitions'. N° d'index: MDE 28/004/1999.*

Amnesty International, 2009. *A Legacy of Impunity: a Threat to Algeria's Future.* Report 28/001/2009.

Belkaïd, Akram, 2005. *Un regard calme sur l'Algérie. Éditions du Seuil.*

Bennoune, Mahfoud, 1988. The Making of Contemporary Algeria, 1830-1987. Cambridge University Press.

Burgis, Tom, 2015. *The Looting Machine: Warlords, Tycoons, Smugglers and the Systematic Theft of Africa's Wealth.* William Collins, London.

Evans, Martin and John Phillips, 2007. *Algeria: Anger of the Dispossessed.* Yale University Press.

Gèze, François, 1998. *Aux origines de la violence. Mouvements, nov-dec '98.* http://www.algeria-watch.org/farticle/tribune/geze2.htm

Gèze, François et Yous, Nesroulah in collaboration with Mellah, Salima, 2000. *Algérie : un témoignage terrifiant,* Postface de *Qui a tué à Bentalha? Algérie: chronique d'un massacre annoncé. La Découverte.*

Gèze, François et Mellah, Salima, 2007. 'Al-Qaida au Maghreb', ou la très étrange *histoire du GSPC algérien:* 1998-2007. Algeria-Watch, http://www.algeria-watch.org/fr/aw/gspc_etrange_histoire.htm. *ok*

Groussard, Serge, 1972. *L'Algérie des adieux. Plon.*

Keenan, Jeremy, 2009. *The Dark Sahara: America's War on Terror in Africa.* Pluto Press.

Keenan, Jeremy, 2013a. *The Dying Sahara: US Imperialism and Terror in Africa.* Pluto Press.

Keenan, Jeremy, 2013b. *A New Phase in the War on Terror?* ISCI report February 2013. http://statecrime.org/data/2014/09/ISCI-Report-February-2013-A-New-Phase-in-the-War-on-

Terror-Jeremy-Keenan.pdf Published by International State Crime Initiative (ISCI), hosted institutionally by Queen Mary University of London.

Kepel, Gilles, 2003. *Jihad: The Trail of Political Islam*. I B Tauris.

Labat, Séverine, 1995. *Les Islamistes algériens. Seuil.*

Laribi, Lyes, 2007. *L'Algérie des généraux. Max Milo Éditions.*

Le Sueur, James D, 2010. *Algeria since 1989: Between Terror and Democracy.* Zed Books.

Malti, Hocine, 2010. *Histoire secrète du pétrole algérien. La Découverte.*

Martinez, Luis, 2000. *The Algerian Civil War.* Hurst & Co, London. Translated by Jonathan Derrick. First published as *La guerre civile en Algérie; Karthala, Paris,* 1998).

Mellah, Salima, 22 September 2007. *Algérie 2003 : L'affaire des « otages du Sahara », décryptage d'une manipulation.* Algeria-Watch, *http://www.algeria-watch.org/fr/aw/otages_sahara.htm*

Power, Jonathan, 2002. *The Story of Amnesty International.* Penguin Books.

Prince, Rob, 2014. *The Tiguentourine Natural Gas Facility Attack in Algeria One Year Later.* Cross-posted from Counterpunch. http://www.counterpunch.org/2014/01/24/tiguentourine-in-amenas-algiers-and-washington-a-year-later/

Reporters sans frontières, 1996. *La drame algérien: Un peuple en otage.* Éditions La *Découverte.*

Roberts, Hugh, 2003. *The Battlefield. Algeria: Studies in a Broken Polity 1988-2002.* Verso.

Robertson, Geoffrey 1999. *Crimes against Humanity.* Allen Lane, The Penguin Press.

Samraoui, Mohammed, 2003. *Chronique des années de sang – Algérie: comment les services secretes ont manipulé les groupes Islamistes. Denoêl Impacts, 2003.*

Schindler, John R, 2012b. *Algeria's Hidden Hand, The National Interest* 22 January 2013 (nationalinterest.org/commentary/algerias-hidden-hand-7994).

Sidhoum, Salah-Eddine and Algeria-Watch, *Algérie:La machine de mort.* Oct 2003.

Sifaoui, Mohamed, 2014. *Histoire secrète de l'Algérie indépendante: L'Etat-DRS. Nouveau monde* éditions.

Souaïdia, Habib, 2001. *La sale guerre.* Éditions La Découverte.

Souaïdia, Habib, 2013: *Révélations sur le drame d'In-Amenas : trente otages* étrangers *tués par l'armée algérienne, au moins neuf militaires tués.* Algeria-Watch, 11 Feb 2013 http://www.algeria-watch.org/fr/aw/souaidia_in_amenas.htm

Stora, Benjamin, 1991. *Histoire de l'Algérié coloniale* (1830-1954). *La Découverte.* (updated 1999).

Stora, Benjamin, 1994. *Histoire de l'Algérie depuis l'indépendance. La Découverte* (updated in 2001).

Stora, Benjamin, 1995. *Histoire de la guerre de l'Algérié* (1954-1962). *La Découverte.*

Stora, Benjamin, 2001. *Histoire de l'Algérié depuis l'indépendance* 1962-1988. *La Découverte.*

Yous, Nesroulah, 2000. *Qui a tué à Bentalha? Algérie: chronique d'un massacre annoncé. La Découverte, Paris.*

Matador

For exclusive discounts on Matador titles,
sign up to our occasional newsletter at
troubador.co.uk/bookshop